Jewish Festivals

TEACHER'S BOOK

Jon Mayled

RMEP

RELIGIOUS AND MORAL EDUCATION PRESS

Religious and Moral Education Press
An Imprint of Wheaton Publishers Ltd
A member of Maxwell Pergamon Publishing Corporation plc
Hennock Road, Exeter EX2 8RP

Pergamon Press Ltd
Headington Hill Hall, Oxford OX3 0BW

Pergamon Press Inc.
Maxwell House, Fairview Park, Elmsford, New York 10523

Pergamon Press Canada Ltd
Suite 104, 150 Consumers Road, Willowdale, Ontario M2J 1P9

Pergamon Press (Australia) Pty Ltd
P.O. Box 544, Potts Point, N.S.W. 2011

Pergamon Press GmbH
Hammerweg 6, D–6242 Kronberg, Federal Republic of
Germany

Copyright © 1988 Jon Mayled

First published 1988

Line illustrations by Mary Suwinski and Ian Foulis & Associates

*Printed in Great Britain by Penwell Ltd, Callington, Cornwall for
A. Wheaton & Co. Ltd, Exeter.*

ISBN 0 08–035101–8

ACKNOWLEDGEMENTS

I wish to acknowledge the help and assistance of my
wife Aviva Paraïso not only by her encouragement but
also in the preparation of the recipes which appear in
this book. I also wish to thank Mrs Binnie Shaw for the
recipe for Pesach biscuits which appears on page 22.

Contents

Introduction

Approaching religions through festivals is an important method in the multifaith classroom and indeed in all classrooms. It provides a dynamic and visible expression to the aspects of both belief and practice in the religion being studied. Because all people, religious and non-religious, celebrate certain events in the year or in their life, it enables religion to be approached through an experience with which the pupil is already partially familiar. Also, in a classroom with a mix of faiths and cultures, or even simply a mix of Christian denominations, it enables a shared experience of mutual learning to take place with its attendant social and educational advantages. In this way no child is excluded from having something to contribute to the study.

The 'concrete' imagery of a religious festival can be used as a peg on which to hang and develop the more complex aspects of religious belief and other significant ideas, such as places of worship and scriptures.

The new Agreed R.E. syllabuses and GCSE syllabuses suggest that festivals have an important part to play in Religious Education, and their introduction into the primary classroom means that Religious Education is seen there as a positive input in their own right. They are also well suited to being revisited in the secondary school. The material in the teacher's books, pupils' books and videos in the *Living Festivals Series* should enable festivals to be approached both systematically and thematically, and it is hoped that they can be handled by those without specialist knowledge of the faith in question, or perhaps of Religious Education teaching itself.

They are also useable within the fields of Integrated Studies and Humanities as they can readily be linked to such subject areas as History, Geography, Social Studies, the Performing Arts, Craft, Design and Technology and Home Economics.

This book, together with the pupils' books and videos, provides the teacher with the basis for a full course on Judaism through the study of festivals. Resources for further study are listed on page 95.

NOTES

1 Throughout this book there are quotations from the Bible. Hebrew quotations are from נביאים וכתובים תורה (Berlin, 1931) and quotations in English from *The Holy Scriptures*, published by the Jewish Publication Society, and *The Apocrypha*, published by Cambridge University Press.

2 Prayers and services are from *The Authorised Daily Prayer Book*, translated by the Rev. S. Singer and published by Eyre and Spottiswoode Ltd (London, 1962).

3 When used in this book the term *Orthodox* generally applies to Orthodox Jewry as represented in Britain by the Chief Rabbi of the United Hebrew Congregations of the British Commonwealth of Nations. Also the terms *Liberal* and *Reform* are employed according to British usage and not American.

4 There is a problem with Hebrew when transliterating into English that there are no exact equivalents to the sounds of Hebrew letters. It would, of course, be possible to use phonetics but here we have followed custom and generally used the standard British transliterations adopted in the Secondary Examinations Council Glossary. In a few cases, one of the alternative spellings listed in the Glossary has been chosen so that, as far as possible, spellings correspond to those found in the *Living Festivals* pupils' books.

For example, the Hebrew character ח Het, is transliterated as 'ch' and pronounced as the 'ch' in the Scottish word 'loch'. This differs from the American usage of simply 'h'.

Judaism

As one of the three 'religions of the Book', Judaism has been included in the work of some R.E. teachers for many years as part of general teaching on Christianity. However, they were often not treating Judaism specifically as a world religion.

With the advent of new Agreed R.E. syllabuses and the GCSE examination, teachers have had to reappraise their approach to Religious Education. This involves a new approach to all world religions, but especially to Christianity and Judaism. In *Christian Festivals* (in this series), we have tried to outline the way in which the traditional approach to the teaching of Christianity can be modified to bring it into line with the treatment of other world faiths. The problem with many earlier treatments of Judaism was that it was regarded as a precursor and preparation for Christianity; almost as a faith which disappeared with the writing of the New Testament and the life of Jesus of Nazareth. It was not given its proper position and full status as a religion in its own right.

With our new approach to world faiths, the time has come to re-evaluate our attitude and approach to Judaism. The GCSE syllabuses are very far-reaching in the coverage required, and touch on many potentially sensitive issues such as Zionism, the State of Israel and the relationship between Christianity and Judaism. However, this should not be permitted to dissuade the teacher from choosing to undertake a study of Judaism.

Judaism and the Jewish people have had a great influence on the cultural, artistic and religious life of Europe and America and this in itself is a worthwhile reason for undertaking a study of the religion.

EARLY HISTORY

Judaism has its roots about 2000 B.C.E. in the city of Ur, in Mesopotamia, now Iraq. According to the Jewish Bible a man called Abraham, who lived in Ur, turned away from the many nature gods of his people and worshipped one god who was known as Yahweh or Jahveh יהוה (see page 9). Abraham made a promise or covenant with this god that he and his family would always worship him and that all the male members of his family would be circumcised as a mark of this covenant. In return, God promised that he would look after the people of Abraham.

The citizens of Ur and the neighbouring cities were merchants and craftsmen and they traded with the cities of Canaan, on the coast of the Mediterranean. Soon, as trade increased, whole families moved to Canaan and took the religion of Abraham with them. According to the Bible, Abraham and his family travelled to Canaan under God's direction.

A trade route was established between Canaan and Egypt. The economy of Egypt was based on agriculture and when Canaan was hit by famine, many people travelled to the land of their trading partners to live. The story of Jacob and Joseph shows how some of these Canaanites reached positions of great importance in Egypt.

An inscription on an Egyptian monument of 1220 B.C.E. refers for the first time to the 'people of Israel'. As we know from the Bible, these Israelites were forced into slavery by the Egyptians and finally, in about 1250 B.C.E., fled from their oppressors under the leadership of Moses. Moses and his brother Aaron led them into the desert of Sinai, and it was here that Moses received the Ten Commandments from God, and re-established the Covenant. The people of Israel accepted Yahweh as their God and their king. After living as nomads in the desert for forty years, the Israelites settled once again in Canaan under the leadership of Joshua, following Moses' death.

The armies of the Philistines invaded the cities of the Canaan from the sea, and the inhabitants fled to join the refugees from Egypt in the countryside. These people were called *apiru* (refugees). This is probably the origin of the word 'Hebrew'.

In the twelfth century B.C.E., the small local communities in the hills and the wilderness of Canaan formed themselves into a federation, and their leaders, such as Gideon, Samuel and Deborah, were known as 'Judges'. As a group they were linked by the Covenant of Sinai.

Later, under attack from the Philistines, they chose a king to lead them. This first king, David, unified the new nation of Israel, and built a city which now lies in ruins outside the south wall of Jerusalem. Here also was built the first Temple to God, where the Ark containing the tablets of stone bearing the Ten Commandments was placed.

The new state of Israel flourished and spread north

to the Euphrates and south to Sinai. David's son, King Solomon, consolidated this power and as the country and people grew rich he fortified the cities of Canaan and built a new Temple in Jerusalem.

After Solomon's death in 920 B.C.E., the kingdom split. In the north was Israel, with a new capital at Samaria, and in the south, Judah with its capital, Jerusalem.

The people turned away from the teachings of Abraham and Moses and from the worship of the one God. Many prophets, such as Amos, Hosea and Isaiah, warned the Israelites that if they did not return to God's ways they would be punished.

In the seventh century B.C.E., Egypt was attacked by the Assyrians and Israel became a vassal state. Then the Babylonians defeated the Egyptians in 605 B.C.E., and Judah was occupied by King Nebuchadnezzar. In 586 B.C.E, 10 000 families were exiled to the city of Babylon and the Jerusalem Temple was destroyed.

It was here in Babylon that the exiled Israelites began the task of writing down the Mosaic law and the history of the Jewish people in the form in which we now have them, the *Torah* (the first five books of the Bible).

At the end of the sixth century B.C.E., Cyrus the Persian conquered all the lands of the Babylonians and ordered the rebuilding of the Temple. In 538 B.C.E., many of the Israelites returned to Jerusalem and under a Jewish nobleman from the Persian court, Nehemiah, the city and the Temple were restored. The Torah was then brought from Babylon to Jerusalem by Ezra.

The Greek general Alexander the Great died in 323 B.C.E., and by this time the influence of Greek culture was felt throughout the Mediterranean. In Egypt many Jews now spoke only Greek and so the Hebrew Bible was translated into the Greek language. This version was known as the *Septuagint* – seventy – because tradition says that seventy translators were employed in its preparation.

Over the next two centuries, large communities of Jews settled at Sardia and Ephesus in Asia Minor and at Alexandria on the coast of Egypt. By the beginning of the second century B.C.E., Judah was ruled by Syria and there were riots in Jerusalem over attempts to make Judaism more Greek. Antiochus, the King of Syria, forced Judaism underground and forbade circumcision and the possession of a copy of the Torah. In 168 B.C.E. he plundered the Temple and ordered pagan sacrifices there. The rebels who still practised Judaism were driven into the hills. There they chose leaders and one of these, Judah (Judas) the Maccabee, led the people as an organized army. They stormed Jerusalem and liberated the Temple. They then established a line of High Priests.

In the first century B.C.E., the Roman Empire spread its influence into Judah, now renamed Judaea. The Romans occupied Jerusalem in 63 B.C.E., and in the year 37 B.C.E. appointed a Jew, Herod, as King of Judaea. He was an Edomite and his Jewishness was disputed. Herod rebuilt the Temple but was hated by the Jews for his heavy taxes and the slavery he enforced on those people who could not pay. On his death in 4 B.C.E., the territory was split between his four sons, one of whom, Herod Antipas, Tetrarch of Peraea and Galilee, is the Herod referred to in the majority of the New Testament.

LATER HISTORY

It was during the period of Roman rule that the idea of the Messiah (q.v.) came to the fore in Jewish thought and teaching. This Messiah would rescue the people from the Romans and restore the Judaean state. There were several revolts during the reign of Herod and his successors and many prophets drew large followings and were claimed as the Messiah. For the Jews, Jesus of Nazareth was seen as one of these.

During the reign of the Emperor Caligula (37–41 C.E.) all Roman subjects were ordered to worship him, and he attempted to erect a statue of himself in the Temple. Conflict between Greeks and Jews continued in the coastal cities of Judaea and the tension between Jews and Romans increased. In 66 C.E. the people rose in a revolt against Rome. At first this was successful, but later there was a crushing defeat and Jerusalem was taken in 70 C.E. The Temple was destroyed and the Jews expelled from Judaea.

The loss of the Temple and of Jerusalem meant that Judaism no longer had a focal and unifying point. A new school of Jewish learning was founded at Jabneh (Jamnia) and the *Rabbis* (masters) replaced the priests as leaders. This school became the organizational centre for Judaism, fixing the calendar for the *Diaspora* – Jews outside Israel. The revolt of the Diaspora in 115–18 C.E. caused disturbances in Palestine which were put down by Lusius Quietus.

There was a further Jewish revolt from 132 to 135 C.E. This was led by Simon bar Kochba, who claimed to be the Messiah. It was put down by Julius Severus and as a consequence, the Emperor Hadrian renamed the country Syria Palaestina, and built a new city of Aelia Capitolina on the site of Jerusalem. The Jews were excluded from Jerusalem and circumcision was forbidden. The centre of Jewish learning moved to Galilee and Antonius Pius (138–61 C.E.) exempted the Jews from the ban on circumcision.

These uprisings in Palestine were echoed in parts of the Diaspora and the Romans persecuted the Jewish communities in Cyprus, Egypt and Cyrenaica (N. Africa). A patriarchate had been established among the Rabbis but was abolished by the Romans in 429 C.E. When the Roman Emperor Constantine converted to Christianity in 313 C.E. it became increasingly difficult for Jews to practise their faith, although it was never made illegal. From the fifth century C.E. relationships between Jews and Persians in Egypt became more difficult and the Jews were ready to welcome the conquering Arabs. Although the Jews helped the Persians invade Palestine in 614 C.E. the uprising in Jerusalem in 617 C.E. was put down by the Byzantine army and the Jews were again expelled from the city.

Many Jews now came under Muslim rule and

prospered in the intellectual world of Islam. Jews in Spain rose to important positions of power in the tenth and eleventh centuries. A type of Judaism known as *Sefardic* developed in this area. The word 'Sefardin' comes from the Hebrew name for Spain, Sefarad. The language of the Sefardi Jews has remained a form of mediaeval Spanish called Ladino.

The Jews elsewhere in Christian Europe were known as *Askenazim* or *Ashkenazi* from Ashkenaz, the Hebrew for Germany. Their language was *Yiddish*, which is a form of mediaeval German with Slavonic and Hebrew additions, and its use has continued since their expulsion from Germany. They were relatively well treated as they supplied the means whereby Christians could borrow money at interest, and so avoid their own religious ban on usury. Many Jews were invited to settle in European countries by the rulers but were expelled when their services were no longer required.

Many Jews were slaughtered as the Crusading armies marched to the 'Holy Land'. The capture of Jerusalem resulted in the burning of many Jews in their synagogues.

During this period Jewish learning continued in Babylon under the Muslims.

Jews entered England in the eleventh century but were expelled in 1290 and did not return until 1650. Between 1290 and 1293 many communities were massacred in southern Italy and many Jews were forced to convert to Christianity. Jews were driven out of France in 1306. They were massacred in 1348 in many countries from Spain to Poland while being blamed for causing the Black Death. This was the time of the 'blood libel', the claim that Jews carry out ritual murder and use the blood of Christian children during Passover.

The Jews of Spain were driven out by fanatical Muslims from north Africa, the *Almohades*, in the twelfth century. The Almohades had arrived to repel an attempted Christian invasion of the country.

The battles between the Spanish kingdoms of Castile and Aragon (1366–9) caused much harm to the Jewish communities in Spain, although especially after the plague of 1348, many Jews were invited back to cities as money-lenders. Anti-Jewish riots flared up in 1391, and many Jews became Marranos (forced converts) and were known as New Christians. However, many of them still kept their beliefs and, as far as possible, their practices. The Spanish Inquisition was set up in 1479 with the approval of the Papacy and was directed against the Marranos – 'pigs' – and Mariscos – 'shell-fish' (Muslim converts to Christianity). However, it soon broke away from Papal control and became a civil institution not abolished until 1808. Under the first inquisitor, at least 2000 people were burnt.

Granada was taken from the Moors in 1492 following the uniting of the two kingdoms by the marriage of King Ferdinand and Queen Isabella and all non-converted Jews were ordered to leave the country by the seventh day of Av in the summer of 1492. Tens of thousands fled as a consequence of this edict, many going to Portugal and Italy while others continued to the Netherlands and some to Israel. By the sixteenth century there were Jewish communities in South America and there were settlements in the Caribbean in 1654.

During the sixteenth and seventeenth centuries the largest numbers of Jews lived in Poland (Lithuania) and the Ottoman Empire. In Poland, the Ukraine and Italy, Jews were again massacred in 1648 and 1649.

In the seventeenth century many Jews moved back into cities of western Europe such as Amsterdam and Paris. There was increasing tolerance rather than acceptance. The consequence of an end to direct persecution was the growth of anti-Semitism. Strong anti-Semite movements developed in Germany and France in the 1880s; this led to massacres – *Pogroms* – and emigration. Also at this time many Jews were driven out of western Russia and went to Europe or North America.

In the period of the Second World War (1939–45) six million Jews were killed by the German Nazis in the notorious concentration camps. This was a third of world Jewry.

In 1948, the State of Israel was created, and many Jews from all over the Diaspora have returned there to live. Today the largest Diaspora community is in the United States of America.

SCRIPTURES

TeNaKh

The Hebrew word *Torah* means 'law' or 'teaching', and the Torah is at the centre of Judaism; it is the word of God. For Jews, the Torah contains the words that God spoke to Moses on Mount Sinai when the Israelites were wandering in the desert. They represent a way of life for the people so that they can live in obedience to God. The scroll on which the Torah is written is central to Jewish worship.

The Jewish Bible is written in Hebrew and the first five books are the Torah: Genesis, Exodus, Leviticus, Numbers and Deuteronomy. This Bible is called in Hebrew the *TeNaKh*: **T**orah (Law), **N**evi'im (Prophets), **K**etuvim (Writings). (Sometimes the whole of the Jewish Bible is referred to as the Torah.) The books of the TeNaKh appear in a slightly different order from those in the Old Testament of the Christian Bible:

TORAH
(*Living Festivals – Shabbat*, p.11 *et seq.*; *Judaism in Words and Pictures*, p.2.)
The Torah is seen as having divine origin as received by Moses from God. There is no idea of evolution in Orthodox Jewish religious ideas, as the Torah contained everything from the Creation. Anything which follows the Torah is not new but a commentary on what is already there.

Torah
  Genesis
  Exodus
  Leviticus
  Numbers
  Deuteronomy

NEVI'IM

This contains stories from the division of the Kingdom to the first return from exile under King Cyrus.

(*Early Prophets*)
Joshua
Judges
I Samuel
II Samuel
I Kings
II Kings

(*Later Prophets*)
Isaiah
Jeremiah
Ezekiel

(*The Twelve*)
Hosea
Joel
Amos
Obadiah
Jonah
Micah
Nahum
Habbakuk
Zephaniah
Haggai
Zechariah
Malachi

KETUVIM

Psalms
Proverbs
Job
Song of Songs
Ruth
Lamentations
Ecclesiastes
Esther
Daniel
Ezra
Nehemiah
I Chronicles
II Chronicles

The scroll of the Torah (used in the synagogue) is known as a *Sefer Torah*. It is handwritten on parchment but does not contain vowels, punctuation or musical notation. In the period 400–1000 C.E. the Masorete scholars devised a system of signs called 'teamim' to show how the Torah should be read and chanted. This is found in printed versions.

Talmud

Talmud means 'teachings', and it is the second most important religious book of the Jews. It is a collection of traditions to explain the Torah together with the Oral Law which was given to Moses and passed down from one generation to another. These traditions and commentaries were written down after the destruction of the Temple and the basic text was completed by the fifth century C.E. It contains the religious laws (*Halachah* in Hebrew) and is a compilation of the work of over a thousand writers. There are sixty-three sections of laws, stories, discussions, parables and history. The non-legal sections are the *Haggadah* (stories); the laws

and rulings are the *Mishnah* (to repeat) and the *Gemara* are the Rabbis' explanations of the law. There are two versions of the Talmud: one written in Babylon (Iraq) and the other in Palestine.

One of the great commentators on the Mishnah was Maimonides (1135–1204), Rabbi Moses ben Maimon. Born in Cordova, he settled in Cairo and wrote the *Mishneh Torah*, a fourteen-part classification of Talmudic teachings.

Midrash

The *Midrash* (the rabbinic commentary and interpretation of the Scriptures) is the third Jewish religious book and contains teachings on law, morality and the religious life based on the Torah. It is also the oldest collection of Jewish stories and legends. It dates from about 200 C.E.

THE IMPORTANCE OF SCRIPTURES

The reading of the Torah is an essential part of worship in the synagogue. It contains not only the Ten Commandments given to Moses on Mount Sinai, but 613 commandments in all, telling how the Jews should live. These commandments are called *mitzvot* (sing. *mitzvah*) and practising Jews follow these to keep the covenant made between God and Moses. If these commandments are obeyed the Jews will be cared for by God; if they are ignored, then the Jews will suffer.

As well as in daily worship and readings from the Torah, the scrolls and the reverence accorded to them play an important part in festival worship.

JEWISH CONCEPT OF GOD

(*Judaism in Words and Pictures*, p.4.)

The Torah says that God made a covenant with Abraham (*c.*1800 B.C.E.) and that in return for worship and obedience God gave the descendants of Abraham protection and the Promised Land of Canaan (Palestine). Thus God directed the course of events and history.

Under the leadership of Moses a further covenant was made whereby the Israelites were to follow the commandments of God:

And the LORD called unto him out of the mountain saying: 'Thus shalt thou say to the house of Jacob, and tell the children of Israel: Ye have seen what I did unto the Egyptians and how I bore you on eagles' wings, and brought you unto Myself. Now therefore, if you will hearken unto My voice indeed, and keep My covenant, then ye shall be Mine own treasure from among all peoples; for all the earth is Mine; and ye shall be unto Me a kingdom of priests and a holy nation'.

Exodus 19:3–6

During the period of the Kings and the division of the Kingdom, God appeared as a forgiving God who nevertheless punished those who turned away from the Covenant. The prophets warned the people of the result of not obeying the mitzvot. They told people God's Will rather than foretelling what would happen in the future. The prophet Ezekiel pointed out that the Jews could not blame their predecessors for God's punishment; the sins of the fathers were not meted on the sons but people were punished for their own wrong-doings.

The existence of God does not need to be proved by miracles as all of Creation is his work. However, because people are created in the image of God they must treat the world and other people as he would do. People must choose for themselves whether they are going to obey God's teachings and commandments or not.

There is no religious community life in Judaism, unlike the religious orders in Christianity, for example. Jews believe that the world was created for people to enjoy – it is not evil and should not be rejected.

The Name of God

The name of the Jewish God is called the *Tetragrammaton*. This refers to the four letters יהוה which transliterated are YHWH or JHVH. The name of God was so sacred that from about 300 B.C.E. it was not spoken when reading the scriptures and instead the word *Adonai*, or Lord, was used. Originally the Torah was 'unpointed': there were no vowels shown, only consonants. When the vowels were put in, those of Adonai were added to the consonants of the Tetragrammaton, thus giving the pronounciation *Jehovah*. The original pronounciation is now thought to have been Yahweh or Jahveh. The origins of the word are obscure. From Psalm 68:4 it appears that it may originally have been 'Yah'. Traditionally it is said to be derived from the verb 'to be'. In Exodus 3:14:

And God said unto Moses; 'I AM THAT I AM'; and He said: 'Thus shalt thou say unto the children of Israel: I AM hath sent me unto you'.

and in Exodus 6:2–3:

And God spoke unto Moses, and said unto him: 'I am the LORD; and I appeared unto Abraham, unto Isaac, and unto Jacob, as God Almighty, but by My name Jehovah, יהוה I made Me not known to them'.

The Messiah

The word Messiah means a person given special powers and functions by God. In Leviticus 4:3 and 5 the priest is described as someone that is anointed. In I Samuel 10:1 and 24:7 the King is called 'the Lord's anointed'. The term was applied to the Davidic dynasty but also to other people such as the patriarchs (I Chronicles 16:22) and even Cyrus (Isaiah 45:1). The idea is contained in Isaiah that there would be a period of rule by the Messiah, who would be of the house of David. This concept arose when the kingdom was threatened by Assyria and Babylon. The idea continued in the writings of Jeremiah and Ezekiel. The Messiah would be chosen by God and after his reign would come the end when everyone would be judged. However, the Messiah would be a human not a divine being.

Various people have claimed to be the Messiah and some, such as Jesus of Nazareth, have been claimed as such by their followers. But the Jews still wait for him to come.

RELIGIOUS LIFE

(*Judaism in Words and Pictures*, p.20.)
There are four rites of passage in Judaism; birth, initiation, marriage and death. The centre of Jewish life is the home and so the main celebration of these events is also there.

There is a different treatment for the rites of passage according to whether the person is male or female, but in recent years in many communities increasing importance has been paid to the woman to give her more equal treatment with the man.

Birth

SHALOM ZACHAR
On the Friday night after a boy is born friends and the Rabbi (religious leader) are often invited to a party to 'greet the male'.

SHALOM NEKEVAH OR *SHALOM BAT*
This is a relatively new custom of 'greeting the female' or 'greeting the daughter' in the same way.

BRIT MILAH

This is My covenant, which ye shall keep, between Me and you and thy seed after thee: every male among you shall be circumcised. And ye shall be circumcised in the flesh of your foreskin; and it shall be a token of a covenant betwixt Me and you. And he that is eight days old shall be circumcised among you, every male throughout your generations...

Genesis 17:10–12

Brit means a covenant and *milah*, circumcision. This ceremony takes place on the eighth day of the boy's life and usually happens at home. It is postponed only if the child is ill and once he has recovered it should take place as soon as possible.

The *kvatterin* is a woman who carries the baby from its mother and hands it to the *kvatter*. He in turn passes the child to the *kiseh shel eliahu*, the man who sits in the chair of Elijah while prayers are said. Finally he hands the boy to the *sandek* or godfather. This man holds the baby while the *mohel* performs the operation. The *mohel* is a Jew specially trained to perform the circumcision.

The mohel says a blessing over a cup of wine and announces, 'Let his name be called in Israel _____, the son of _____'. The baby is then given a small drop of wine. After this there will be a party to celebrate.

SIMCHAT HABAT

There is no such ceremony for a baby girl but in the synagogue on the Sabbath after her birth the father is called up to offer a blessing:

He Who blessed our fathers Abraham, Isaac and Jacob, Moses and Aaron, David and Solomon, may he bless the mother _____ and her newborn daughter, whose name in Israel shall be called _____. May they raise her for the marriage canopy and for a life of good deeds, and let us say Amen.

Today there are often more elaborate ceremonies for the birth of a girl and the child may be carried into the synagogue.

The names given to children will usually include a Biblical name in Hebrew and also, in the case of Ashkenazi Jews, that of a dead relative or friend. Generally, children are not named after living people except in the case of Sefardim.

PIDYON HABEN

This is the final part of the birth ceremonies.

And the Lord spoke unto Moses, saying: 'Sanctify unto Me all the first-born, whatsoever openeth the womb among the children of Israel, both of man and of beast, it is Mine'.

Exodus 13:1–2

This was the original instruction given by God to the Israelites but after they had made and worshipped the golden calf in the wilderness while Moses was talking with God on Mount Sinai, this instruction was given:

And I have taken the Levites instead of the first-born among the children of Israel.

Numbers 8:18

The first-born ... from a month old shall you redeem ... Their redemption money shall be the value of five shekels of silver.

Numbers 18:15–16

So every first-born male child (without the woman having had a miscarriage after three months of pregnancy or the birth being by Caesarian section) has to be redeemed by a Cohen (a Jew of priestly descent). This does not apply if one of the parents is of the family of Levi or Cohen.

A short service takes place in the home where the child is offered to a Cohen and then bought back for five silver shekels. Special silver coins are now struck by the Israeli government for use at the ceremony. The money is then donated to charity.

Initiation

BAR MITZVAH

The Jewish initiation ceremony – Bar Mitzvah – is *not* a mitzvah. It is a tradition that when a boy reaches the age of thirteen he is responsible for his own actions and can be fully responsible for fulfilling the commandments. It means Son (Bar) of the Commandment

(Mitzvah). A boy *has* a Bar Mitzvah; he is not Bar Mitzvahed.

The boy is taught how to put on – 'lay' – tefillin (q.v.) and to read Hebrew. He prepares a 'portion', a passage that he will read in the synagogue. Originally he had simply to recite the Torah blessings after the reading:

Blessed are You, Lord our God, King of the universe, who has given us the Law of truth, and hast planted everlasting life in our midst. Blessed art thou, O Lord, who givest the Law.

After the synagogue service where he is called up to read, his father says:

Blessed be He Who has released me from the responsibilities of this child.

The ceremony is usually followed by a party and the boy receives presents and cards.

BAT MITZVAH

Today there is an increasing trend in some communities for girls to have an initiation ceremony at the age of twelve. *Bat Mitzvah* means Daughter of the Commandment. The ceremony is very similar to that for a boy but the girl does not learn the laying of tefillin, etc.

Marriage

The Jewish family and home is the centre of religious life and marriage therefore has a corresponding importance. Many things have changed in recent years and few people employ a *shadchan* or matchmaker to find suitable partners for their children. In the same way people do not always become formally engaged by *t'naim*, the signing of a formal contract for marriage.

The service can take place anywhere provided that the couple are married under a *chuppah* or canopy. Before the ceremony begins, two male witnesses sign a contract or *ketubah* saying what duties each partner will undertake as husband or wife. The text of the ketubah dates from the second or third century B.C.E., and is written in Aramaic.

Before the wedding the bride will take a special ritual bath in a *mikvah* so that she is ritually purified. She and the groom do not see one another for a week before the wedding.

The bride and groom are each brought to the chuppah by their parents. Before the ceremony begins the groom may put on a *kittel*, a pure white gown symbolizing purity. The bride walks around the groom seven times and stands on his right facing the Rabbi.

The Rabbi says a blessing over a cup of wine and the bride and groom drink from it. Then the groom places a plain gold ring on the first finger of the bride's right hand and says in Hebrew:

Be sanctified to me with this ring in accordance with the law of Moses and Israel.

The ketubah is then read aloud and handed by the groom to his bride. This is followed by seven blessings over another cup of wine.

Finally there is a reminder that the Temple is destroyed and that Jews have been scattered all over the world: a glass is wrapped in a cloth and the groom smashes it under his foot.

DIVORCE

Divorce is permitted in Judaism and may be encouraged rather than that two people should live together unhappily. The Jewish court or *Beth Din* will grant a divorce or *get* if the two people agree.

Death

As soon as someone dies preparations must be made for burial; if possible on the same day but if not then on the following one. The *Chevra Kadisha* (Sacred Burial Society) go to the undertakers and prepare the body. The dead person must be washed and dressed in a plain white shroud or *tachrichim*. If it is a man then he wears his tallit but the fringes are cut to show that he is now free of mitzvot. Jewish law requires a plain pine coffin and this is sealed as soon as the body is placed inside. A dead person is never left alone from the time of death until the burial.

Immediately before the burial the mourners will make a tear in their garments – *keriah* – to show their grief. There are no flowers at a Jewish funeral and the service is short and simple. (Cremation is not usually permitted amongst Orthodox Jews.)

After burial the traditional blessing is said:

May God comfort you among all the mourners of Zion and Jerusalem.

A Cohen is not allowed to enter a funeral parlour or cemetery except for the burial of one of seven immediate relatives.

After the funeral the family go home to sit *Shiva* (Hebrew – 'seven'). Throughout the seven days a candle is kept burning and the mirrors in the house are covered. The mourners do not leave their homes: they do not shave or cut their hair and they sit on low stools. They say *Kaddish* (prayer for the dead) three times a day and the community will come to the house to say it with them. Shiva is broken only by the Sabbath or a Jewish festival which must take precedence. The thirty days after burial are the period of *Shloshim*, when bereaved avoid going out for pleasure and continue to mourn. For the next eleven months, *Shanah* (but no longer), Kaddish is said every day. After this time the dead person is remembered each year on the anniversary of death by the lighting of a *yahrzeit* candle which burns for a full day, and by the reciting of Kaddish.

PLACE OF WORSHIP

The principal Jewish place of worship is the home and this is examined in more detail in the chapters on the individual festivals. However, the central place for community worship is the **synagogue**.

Synagogue

(*Judaism in Words and Pictures*, pp.10 and 16; *Living Festivals – Shabbat*, p.23 *et seq.*)

During the period following the rebuilding of the Temple in Jerusalem there grew up the *Beth Hamidrash* (house of learning) where people met to study the scriptures. Following the destruction of the Temple, sacrifices could no longer be made, so they were replaced by prayer. The only places available for Jews to worship were the synagogues – συναγωγη (Greek for 'bringing together') or, in Hebrew, *Beth ha Knesset* (house of assembly). The prayers are printed in a book called a *siddur*.

The synagogue is not only a place of prayer but also a centre for the social and cultural life of the community and it often houses the *cheder* (room), the religious school.

From the outside synagogues are plain buildings often with no more decoration than the *Magen David* (star of David) to show their use.

The interiors of all synagogues have similar features. There are no pictures or statues in a synagogue in accordance with the second commandment. In the eastern wall (*mizrach*) is the *Aron Ha-Kodesh*, the Holy Ark. This is set to face Jerusalem and contains the *Sefer Torah* (Torah scroll).

The scrolls are on two wooden rollers (*Etz chaim* – the trees of life) with silver crowns (*keter*) and bells (*rimmonim* – pomegranates). They have velvet covers and an ornate breast-plate (*tas*) representing the one worn by the High Priest.

In front of the ark is the *parochet* or curtain (Exodus 26:31–34). Above the ark are two tablets bearing the first two words of each of the Ten Commandments. Also, in front of the ark may be the verse:

Know before whom you are standing.

Above the ark burns the *Ner Tamid*, the everlasting light. This represents the lamp which burnt in the Temple in Jerusalem (Exodus 27:20–21). On or above the parochet may be the Lions of Judah (Genesis 49:9) and a crown (*Keter Torah*): for Jews the Torah is the crowning glory which God gave to the world. Also at the east end of the synagogue may stand a *menorah*, a seven-branched candlestick representing the one which stood in the Temple.

In an Orthodox synagogue men and women sit separately; the women usually sit in a gallery. In the centre of the room is the *bimah*, a stand from where the Torah is read. When the scrolls are being read, the reader follows the line of script with a silver pointer shaped like a hand; this is called a *yad* and hangs over the top of the wooden rollers when the scrolls are in the ark. The *chazzan* (a singer) leads the worship.

The sermon on a Sabbath morning will be given by the Rabbi (teacher), who is not a priest, but the leader and teacher of the local community. A group of Rabbis forms the Beth Din for the area; this supervises all matters relating to Jewish law especially food (q.v.).

For any service to take place there must be a minimum of ten adult males (*minyan*). During the service men will wear their kapels or kipot (sing. kipah) and, at a morning service, tallits. (Tallits are worn at an evening service only on Yom Kippur – see page 57.) In an Orthodox synagogue the service will be in Hebrew.

The service consists mainly of prayers and the central reading of the Torah, the whole of which is read at Sabbath services during the course of each year (see page 68).

Home

The Jewish home is a very special place. It has a kitchen specially equipped for cooking kosher food (q.v.). In addition it will have a *mezuzah* at each door. The mezuzah is a small cylinder fixed to the top of the right-hand door-post as you enter a room. It contains a piece of parchment on which is written sacred passages from the Torah:

HEAR, O ISRAEL: THE LORD OUR GOD, THE LORD IS ONE. And thou shalt love the LORD thy God with all they heart, and with all thy soul, and with all thy might. And these words, which I command thee this day, shall be upon thy heart; and thou shalt teach them diligently unto thy children, and shalt talk of them when thou sittest in thy house, and when thou walkest by the way, and when thou liest down, and when thou risest up. And thou shalt bind them for a sign upon thy hand, and they shall be for frontlets between thine eyes. And thou shalt write them upon the door-posts of thy house, and upon thy gates.

Deuteronomy 6:4–9
and **Deuteronomy 11:13–21**

As they pass in and out Jews touch the mezuzah and take their fingers to their lips. The first part of this passage is known as the *Shema* (hear).

FOOD LAWS

The books Leviticus and Deuteronomy give various food laws which are still strictly adhered to by Orthodox Jews today (Leviticus 11, Deuteronomy 14).

The technical word for food which Jews can eat is *kasher* – permitted (usually spelt and pronounced *kosher*). Food which they cannot eat is *terefah* – forbidden.

Provided that it is slaughtered by a ritual method known as *schechitah*, Jews may eat the meat or meat products of animals which have both cloven hooves and chew the cud. This of course excludes pork. Also the sciatic nerve is forbidden (Genesis 32:33, Leviticus 7:25) and in Britain only the fore-quarters of animals are kosher. In other countries the arteries and sinews of the hind-quarters are sometimes removed so that they may be eaten. But this is a complicated operation and usually the hind-quarters are sent to a non-kosher butcher. There are several Jewish slaughterhouses in Britain.

Shechitah is performed by a *schochet*. He says a blessing and then, with a very sharp knife, kills the animal with a single cut across the throat. The animal is hung upside down for the blood to drain out. Following this the meat has to be checked for disease. The presence of blood or disease after slaughter renders the meat terefah. In addition the meat has to be soaked and salted before cooking to remove any

remaining blood. The purpose of this form of slaughter is to cause as little suffering as possible. The animal is not kosher if it does not die immediately from the single cut.

Fish with scales, fins and a backbone are permitted, but shellfish are not. Likewise, certain types of birds such as chicken are allowed if they are slaughtered correctly.

Meat and dairy products may not be eaten or cooked together and separate cooking utensils are used.

Thou shalt not seethe a kid in its mother's milk.

Deuteronomy 14:21

This means that there are three different types of food:

1 **Meat** (fleischig): this covers all kosher meat and meat products.

2 **Milk** (milchig): all milk and milk products – of course hard cheese made with animal rennet is not permitted.

3 **Parev** or **Parve**: these are all foods which are not meat or milk such as eggs (these must be checked for bloodspots before using), vegetables, fruits, cereals, beans and pulses, fish and according to the Bible, locusts. Honey is also included in this group – although the bee itself is not kosher the argument is that the honey is never actually part of the bee but merely carried by it.

Although meat and milk may not be mixed, parve food can be eaten with either. Jewish kitchens should have three sets of cooking utensils, one for each food group, and two sets of crockery and cutlery for daily use (as well as additional festival sets). In practice however, most people do not keep a special parve set of utensils and instead cook parve food in the utensils pertaining to the rest of the meal.

The mitzvah covering meat and milk requires that an interval of between 1 and 6 hours must elapse (depending on the particular Jewish community) between eating meat and following it with milk. This allows any particles or aftertaste to leave the mouth. It is also usual to leave the same time gap between eating hard cheese (made without animal rennet) and following it with meat. But after other milk foods, it is only necessary to wash the mouth and hands thoroughly before eating meat. Again many Jews leave a gap of 3 hours between these products anyway.

Although fish is regarded as parve it is not eaten with meat, e.g. meat with a fish sauce. This was originally for health reasons and is a mediaeval ruling: Tur: Yoreh Deah 87; Shulchan Arukh: Yoreh Deah 87:3 (Talmud).

These requirements of Jewish food laws have led in some communities to the development of a kosher cuisine. Some principles of this cuisine among Ashkenazi (Eastern European) Jews, namely a high intake of fat and sugar, are at variance with those of modern dietary practice but are part of the Jewish way of life. As such they should be recognized as being, for these

Jews, as much a part of their culture as those of any other religious or cultural group. However, a high intake of fat and sugar often results in diabetes and coronary heart disease in later life. This is a very serious health problem in Israel today.

The tradition of Jewish food is not based on that of the homeland of Israel. The land of Israel has largely been irrigated and is once again fertile and grows many fruits. But the tradition of Jewish food which we have today is largely Eastern European in origin. Foods which are traditionally thought of as Jewish, bagels, salt beef and cheesecake, owe their origins to the Diaspora.

The preparation of kosher food outside the home, such as by butchers and restaurants, comes under the supervision of the Beth Din and food which is approved as kosher bears the stamp of the local Beth Din authority.

RELIGIOUS DRESS

There are three principal articles of Jewish dress which are worn by men:

KAPEL, KIPPAH OR YAMULKA
This is the skull-cap often worn all the time by Orthodox Jews. It can be made of almost any material and may be embroidered. It is a reminder that the wearer is always in the presence of God.

TEFILLIN OR PHYLACTERIES
In accordance with Exodus 6:9, Jewish men 'lay tefillin' before morning prayer on weekdays (tefillin are not worn on the Sabbath). They are two small, black, leather boxes with thongs, the *shel yad* and the *shel rosh*. They contain parchment on which is written Exodus 13:1–10 and 11–16, and Deuteronomy 6:4–9 and 11:13–21. The shel yad is put on first with the *bayit* or box on the biceps muscle of the arm. The strap is wound around the arm seven times. Then the shel rosh is tied on the forehead between the eyes with a knot at the nape of the neck. The strap of the shel yad is then tied around the hand.

TALLIT
The tallit or prayer shawl is worn every day for morning prayer. It is a long fringed shawl (usually white) with blue or black stripes. The fringes make eight strands and five knots at each corner. These fringes are called *tzizit* and in the Hebrew numbering system the letters of tzizit are equal to 600;

$$600 + 8 \text{ (strands)} + 5 \text{ (knots)} = 613.$$

There are 613 commandments in the Torah.

Some Orthodox Jews wear an undergarment called a tzizit or *tallit katan* at all times. It is shaped like a tabard and the fringes are often visible under the shirt.

There are no particular dress requirements for women. However, some Orthodox women wear a *sheitel* to cover their hair. This may be a scarf or hat but in more recent times, it is often a wig.

Because of a commandment not to cut the corners of their hair, some Jews allow the hair in front of their ears to grow down into *payes* (Hebrew 'pe'ot').

Prayer
There are three daily periods of prayer:
early morning – *shacharit*
afternoon – *mincha*
evening – *ma-ariv*.
All prayers are said facing East, towards, Israel.

Pilgrimage
In the times of the Temple, Passover, Shavuot and Succot were the three pilgrim festivals when people tried to get to Jerusalem to offer a sacrifice. With the destruction of the Temple this ceased. Today, organized pilgrimage in Judaism is rare. However, many Jews from the Diaspora visit Israel and often travel to the Western Wall to pray. (This wall is not part of the Temple but a remaining fragment of the foundations of the Temple mount from the time of Herod.)

Many Jews now also make a pilgrimage to the Memorial of the Holocaust in Jerusalem, *Yad Vashem* – a place and a name.

JEWISH SECTS

Throughout this book we continually refer to Orthodox Judaism, by which we mean the traditions of Ashkenazi and Sefardi Jews, who are the single largest group in Jewry today. However, there are other Jewish sects and traditions in the world.

ASHKENAZI JEWS
This name is derived from Ashkenaz, the great-grandson of Noah (Genesis 10:3), who is said to have settled in what is now called Germany. The name has therefore come to apply to all Jews from Eastern and Central Europe. [For a very different discussion about the origin of the Ashkenazi see *The Thirteenth Tribe*, by Arthur Koestler, Picador, 1976.]

SEFARDI JEWS
These are the Spanish and Portuguese Jews who were driven out of Spain in 1492.

These two groups have developed different traditions, both being influenced by the countries in which they lived: the Ashkenazi by Christian Germany; the Sefardim by Muslim Spain. Today the Sefardim make up only 17 per cent of world Jewry though half of the population of Israel.

KABBALISTIC JEWS
Some Sefardim in Spain studied esoteric interpretations of the Holy Scriptures in the thirteenth and fourteenth centuries. As a result, they developed a form of mystical Judaism incorporating aspects of astrology.

ORIENTAL JEWS
Many Jewish communities have lived in the Middle East since the time of the Temple and maintain their own traditions and cultures.

HASIDIC JEWS

Hasid means pious and this mystical form of Judaism developed in Poland in the eighteenth century. Its founder, Baal Shem Tov, followed the teachings of a book called the *Zorah* (splendour) used by the Kabbalistic Sefardi and called for a highly passionate and ecstatic form of worship. It was Judaism through feeling rather than study. The spiritual leaders of the Hasidim are called *zaddikim* (saints) and the community teachers, *rebbes*. They are extremely orthodox and traditional in their dress and ritual observance.

REFORM JEWS

In the eighteenth century, German Jewish intellectuals argued for changes to Judaism, so that while it still remained traditional it was more acceptable in Gentile society. Moses Mendelssohn translated the scriptures into German and attempted to improve people's knowledge of Hebrew and the Jewish moral values.

From 1810 Israel Jacobson introduced changes in the liturgy: a sermon in the vernacular, organ music and shorter prayers. There have been both moderate reformers such as Abraham Geiger and more radical reformers such as Samuel Holdheim. The first Reform congregation was founded in Britain in 1840. In most Reform communities men and women sit together to worship.

LIBERAL JUDAISM

A more radical approach to reform came to Britain in 1902 with the foundation of Liberal Judaism. Its early members included Claude Montefiore and Lilian Montague. Many changes were proposed such as the moving of Sabbath services from Saturday to Sunday and a rejection of Zionism as being a negation of Jewish universalism.

Today the Liberal or Reform communities may have women Rabbis.

ORTHODOX JEWS

The principle of Orthodox Jewry is to live strictly by the mitzvot of the Torah, which they believe is a once and for all revelation direct from God. The majority of British Jews are Orthodox under the Chief Rabbi of the United Hebrew Congregations of the Commonwealth. The establishment of a community of Orthodox Jews was a further reaction to the Liberal movement. Rabbi Samson Raphael Hirsch (1810–88) acknowledged that Jews live in a modern world which they should study and take part in, but by doing so they should not compromise on the observance of the mitzvot.

ZIONISTS

In Basle in 1897, Theodore Herzl called for the establishment of Eretz Israel (the land of Israel) as a Jewish state. Some Orthodox Jews refused to support this, saying that Israel could not be reborn until the Messiah returned. Also other, Liberal Jews saw no purpose in returning to Israel. However, after much bitter argument and fighting the State of Israel was founded in 1948.

14

YIDDISH

A language spoken by Jews, based on ancient or provincial German with Hebrew and Slavonic additions ... (Chambers 20th Century Dictionary)

As more Jews have absorbed much of the culture of the countries in which they live Yiddish is now rarely spoken as a language. It has however given some words to the English language and some particular words and phrases are often used still by Jews in Britain.

Here are a few examples of words which may often be heard:

bagel – ring-shaped bread roll
borsht – beetroot soup
frum – a religious person
gelt – money
goy – gentile
kapel – yarmulka (skull cap)
kinder – children
klutz – clumsy person
mazel tov! – congratulations
nosh – food (eaten between meals)
putz – stupid person
shabbes – Sabbath
shlep – to walk (a long way)
shmaltz – sentimentality
shmatta – rubbish
sholem – peace
shtook – trouble
shul – synagogue
shyster – crook
spiel – talk
worsht – salami

APPROACHES TO JUDAISM THROUGH FESTIVALS

The festivals of Judaism mark the agricultural year of the Jewish homeland and commemorate events of the Bible. Bringing these times of rejoicing and remembrance into the home gives them added significance.

Judaism, by focusing on the observances, makes the celebration of the yearly festivals part of family life. The most important event is the Sabbath and its observation brings the religion into a particular prominence. A study of the yearly cycle of festivals together with the weekly Sabbath brings to the foreground many of the essential beliefs and observances which are central to Jewish life.

It is the observance of the mitzvot which has enabled Jews in the Diaspora to maintain a common culture regardless of the part of the world in which they live. Jewish festivals have not attracted any significant commercialism and are therefore celebrated because of what they are. The average Jewish family, however far it may have lapsed from Orthodoxy, will in all probability still meet together to observe the most important of these yearly events.

As the festivals are such an important part of family life and as the family is central to Judaism, they are an excellent point at which to begin a study of this faith.

Festivals in Judaism

THE JEWISH CALENDAR

Judaism may have given the world the seven-day week based on the account of Creation in the Book of Genesis, but we have to remember that the Jewish day begins at sunset. For example, the Sabbath, Shabbat, begins at sunset on Friday and ends at sunset on Saturday. The Jewish day always begins with sunset because the account of the Creation in Genesis states:

And there was evening and there was morning, one day.

Genesis 1:5

The Jewish calendar is lunisolar and so it is not possible to draw parallels with the Gregorian months. As an approximation, Nisan marks the beginning of Spring. A new month begins with a new moon.

Jewish Months:

1st	Nisan	30 days
2nd	Iyar	29 days
3rd	Sivan	30 days
4th	Tammuz	29 days
5th	Av	30 days
6th	Elul	29 days
7th	Tishri	30 days
8th	Heshvan	29 or 30 days
9th	Kislev	29 or 30 days
10th	Tevet	29 days
11th	Shevat	30 days
12th	Adar	29 days (Leap Year 30 days)
13th	Adar II	29 days (Leap Year)

A lunar month is counted as either 29 or 30 days and in a lunar year there are 354 days. But for the implementation of leap years, after three years the calendar would be 33 days behind the sun. Thus in leap years the extra month of Adar II is added and this then fits into a nineteen-year cycle of seven leap years. Adar II is added in the third, sixth, eighth, eleventh, fourteenth, seventeenth and nineteenth years.

The chart on page 16 shows the major Jewish festivals. The first column indicates the month and day(s) on which the festival is celebrated according to the Hebrew calendar. Although the Jewish New Year, Rosh Hashanah, is celebrated at the beginning of the month of Tishri in September, the actual months are numbered from Nisan, which starts in March.

The second column gives the name of the festival, beginning with Passover and ending with Purim.

The third column shows the approximate western month according to the Gregorian calendar.

Finally, the fourth column gives the origins of the festivals. These are divided into four categories: Biblical – listed in Leviticus 23: 1–44; Rabbinic – found in the Talmud; Mediaeval, and Modern.

Major festivals are known as *Yom Tov* – good day. The two principal festivals, the High Holy Days, are Rosh Hashanah (New Year) and Yom Kippur (the Day of Atonement). Passover, Shavuot and Succot are the three pilgrim festivals. The major festivals are dealt with later in this book and in *Living Festivals* pupils' books. Some of the minor festivals are also dealt with later in this book; details of the others are given here.

Yom Hashoah – this recalls the six million Jews who died in the Holocaust during the Second World War.

Yom Hazikaron – this is Israel Remembrance Day, when all those who have died in the defence of Israel are remembered.

Yom Ha'Atzmaut – Independence Day, the anniversary of the establishment of the State of Israel in 1948.

Lag B'Omer – this is a break in the counting of Omer from Passover to Shavuot. It is a students' holiday and three-year-old boys have their first haircut.

Yom Yerushalayim – this marks the third day of the Six Day War in 1967, when Jews returned to the Old City of Jerusalem after nineteen years.

Shivah Asar B'Tammuz – the day on which Moses came down from Mount Sinai and saw the golden calf.

Tisha B'Av – possibly the summer equivalent of Tu B'Shevat. It is a day when many tragedies in Jewish history are said to have occurred.

Tzom Gedaliah – the murder of Gedaliah, who had been appointed as Jewish Governor by Nebuchadnezzar. The remaining Jews fled to Egypt.

Asarah B'Tevet – the day that Nebuchadnezzar besieged Jerusalem. The fast cannot be postponed even if it falls on Shabbat and so the calendar is arranged in order that Shabbat cannot fall on this day.

Hebrew dates	Festival	Secular month	Origin
15–22 Nisan	Passover	March–April	Biblical
16 Nisan – 5 Sivan	Counting of Omer	April–June	Biblical
27 Nisan	Yom Hashoah (Holocaust Day)	April–May	Modern
4 Iyar	Yom Hazikaron (Israel Day)	April–May	Modern
5 Iyar	Yom Ha'Atzmaut (Israel Ind. Day)	April–May	Modern
18 Iyar	Lag B'Omer	May	Rabbinic
28 Iyar	Yom Yerushalayim (Jerusalem Day)	May–June	Modern
6–7 Sivan	Shavuot	May–June	Biblical
17 Tammuz	Shivah Asar B'Tammuz	July	Rabbinic
9 Av	Tisha B'Av	July–August	Rabbinic
1–29 Elul	Teshuvah (month of repentance)	August–September	Rabbinic
1–2 Tishri	Rosh Hashanah	September	Biblical
3 Tishri	Tzom Gedaliah	September	Rabbinic
10 Tishri	Yom Kippur	Sept–Oct	Biblical
15–22 Tishri	Succot	Sept–Oct	Biblical
22 Tishri	Shemini Atseret	Sept–Oct	Biblical
23 Tishri	Simchat Torah	Sept–Oct	Mediaeval
25 Kislev	Chanukah	December	Rabbinic
10 Tevet	Asarah B'Tevet	January	Rabbinic
15 Shevat	Tu B'Shevat	Jan–Feb	Rabbinic
13 Adar	Ta'anit Esther	Feb–March	Rabbinic
14 Adar	Purim	Feb–March	Rabbinic

THE FESTIVALS

The festivals covered in this book are those dealt with in the *Living Festivals* series: *Shabbat, Passover, Rosh Hashanah and Yom Kippur, Succot and Simchat Torah, Chanukah.* In addition the festivals of Shemini Atseret, Tu B'Shevat, Shavuot and Purim are covered as they appear in some of the GCSE syllabuses.

Starting with Shabbat, the pattern in this book then follows the Jewish year beginning with Passover and concluding with Purim. The section on each festival is divided into two main parts:

Themes: this provides a general introduction to the festival for the teacher based closely on the *Living Festivals Series* pupils' books and, where appropriate, one of the videos. Each section on themes has been structured in the following way:

1 an introduction to the festival.

2 the various aspects of the festival arranged in a common format:
   (a) Stories and legends with their sources and dates (all dates are of course approximate).
   (b) Location.
   (c) Ritual.
   (d) Artefacts.
   (e) Food.
   (f) Significant persons.

3 suggested themes for use in the classroom (these include some references to the celebrations of these festivals held in various Jewish sects).

Note: These structured analyses of themes are not intended in any way to provide all the necessary information for a study of the festival. They are designed to provide guidelines and a checklist for each festival which will point the way to original sources or other information which the teacher may wish to use.

Worksheets: there are worksheets for each of the festivals in addition to the general ones on Judaism. It is hoped that these will provide sufficient material and ideas for the teacher to cover the festival fully. They can of course be adapted to suit the individual requirements of the teacher and class. The idea is that the general sheets should be selected by the teacher to use with whatever festival is being studied.

These worksheets are not intended to be used as a full set. They have been designed for different ability ranges and different ages.

They are in three sections:

1 factual information on the festival obtained from the books and videos.

2 practical work: this may include cross-curricular materials extending into such areas as Home Economics (Food Studies and Textiles), Art, Geography, Music and Drama. It is of course up to the individual teacher whether this work is tackled in the R.E. classroom or whether it is used to establish cross-curricular links with other departments.

Calendar of Jewish Holy Days

FESTIVALS		1988	1989	1990	1991	1992	1993	1994
Passover								
	1st day	2 Apr	20 Apr	10 Apr	30 Mar	18 Apr	6 Apr	27 Mar
	2nd day	3 Apr	21 Apr	11 Apr	31 Mar	19 Apr	7 Apr	28 Mar
	7th day	8 Apr	26 Apr	16 Apr	5 Apr	20 Apr	12 Apr	2 Apr
	8th day	9 Apr	27 Apr	17 Apr	6 Apr	21 Apr	13 Apr	3Apr
Shavuot								
	1st day	22 May	9 Jun	30 May	19 May	7 Jun	26 May	16 May
	2nd day	23 May	10 Jun	31 May	20 May	8 Jun	27 May	17 May
Rosh Hashanah								
	1st day	12 Sep	30 Sep	20 Sep	9 Sep	28 Sep	16 Sep	6 Sep
	2nd day	13 Sep	1 Oct	21 Sep	10 Sep	29 Sep	17 Sep	7 Sep
Yom Kippur		21 Sep	9 Oct	29 Sep	18 Sep	7 Oct	25 Sep	15 Sep
Succot								
	1st day	26 Sep	14 Oct	4 Oct	23 Sep	12 Oct	30 Sep	20 Sep
	2nd day	27 Sep	15 Oct	5 Oct	24 Sep	13 Oct	1 Oct	21 Sep
(Shemini Atseret)								
	8th day	3 Oct	21 Oct	11 Oct	30 Sep	19 Oct	7 Oct	27 Sep
(Simchat Torah)								
	9th day	4 Oct	22 Oct	12 Oct	1 Oct	20 Oct	8 Oct	28 Sep

3 puzzles based on the festival. The wordsquares require more thought than the wordsearches but some pupils may find them easier. They both serve to strengthen knowledge of words associated with the religion and the festival.

4 each group concludes with two sheets of assessments. One is in the form of a short test for younger children while the second is a graded assessment which should provide questions up to examination level.

The questions are of varying levels of difficulty and are designed to help the teacher assess what concepts and skills have been developed in the particular study. Some of the questions may also be used separately for project work.

No attempt has been made in either the themes or the worksheets to delineate what is to be used in the Junior, Middle or Secondary school. The teacher is a professional who is well able to choose and adapt the material to the needs and abilities of the pupils. Some of the practical work is comparatively complex and may require skills and techniques which the younger pupil does not have but again it is for the teacher to decide.

THE WORKSHEETS

The first worksheet is a research task based on a map of world Jewry. (The *Encyclopaedia Britannica* is a useful source book for this exercise.) The second deals with symbols of Judaism.

The next seven are orientated to Home Economics. There are simple instructions for making a kapel (as an alternative, there is a pattern for a crochet kapel in the *Jewish Catalog* p. 49-50) and then a sheet on Jewish food laws. This is followed by five recipes. The first two – Yemenite charoset and Pesach biscuits – are examples of Passover cookery. The cheesecake is a traditional Ashkenazi recipe for Shavuot and this is followed by tzimmes for Rosh Hashanah and latkes for Chanukah.

Next there is a Wordsquare on Judaism.

The final two worksheets are a test and a full assessment.

MAP OF WORLD JEWRY

1 Mark Israel on the map.

2 Today there are Diaspora Jews all over the world. Show on the map where major Jewish communities have been established and, where possible, give dates for these.

SYMBOLS

On this page there are pictures of seven important Jewish objects. Work out what each one is and write the name beside the picture. Then write one or two sentences saying what each one represents or is used for. Finally, colour in the pictures.

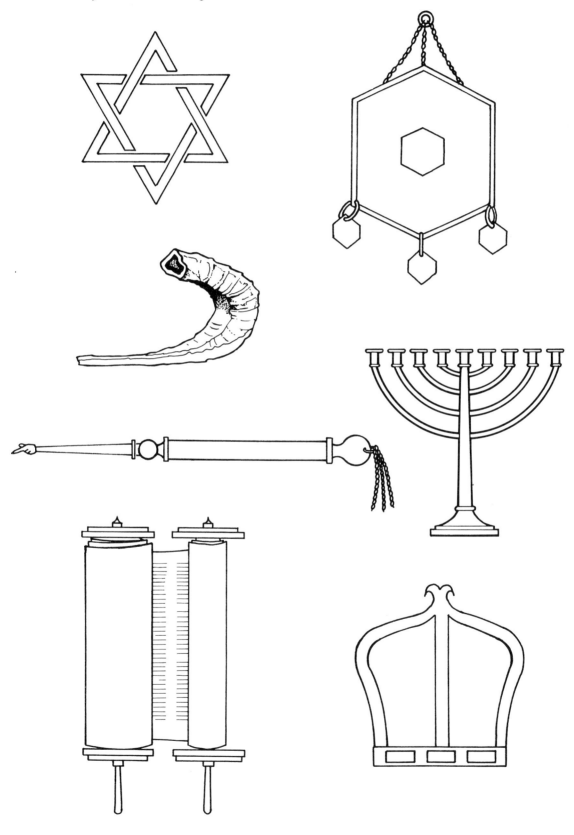

MAKING A KAPEL

This picture shows two objects to do with Jewish dress: what are they?

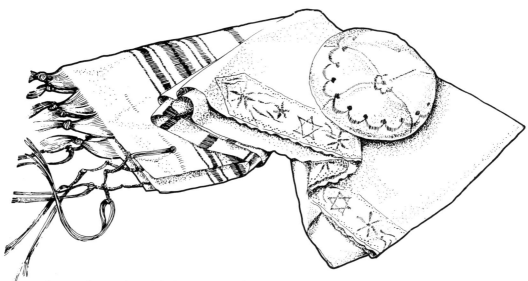

What colour should the stripes be?

These are the instructions for making a kapel but there are many different ways in which these can be made and decorated.

MATERIALS
    large empty wooden cotton reel
    four nails and a hammer
    (*or* use a ready-made French-knitting kit)
    crochet hook
    needle and cotton
    wool

1 Place the four nails around the hole at one end of the cotton reel. Knock them in so that at least 10 mm is still showing.

2 Drop one end of the wool through the hole and then wind the wool twice around the nails.

3 With the crochet hook lift the bottom strand over the top by each nail. Continue to wind the wool around and to lift each strand over. Soon a long woollen tube will begin to appear through the hole at the bottom of the reel.

4 As it appears, wind it into a spiral. When the spiral is about 125–150 mm across, cut the wool. Take it off the nails and sew in the ends.

5 With a needle and cotton sew the spiral together. If you do this carefully you can make it into a round-domed cap.

6 Now you can embroider a pattern around the edge in a contrasting colour.

Kapels are kept in place with hair-grips!

FOOD LAWS

Read: **Leviticus 11**
        Deuteronomy 14
        Leviticus 7:25
        Genesis 32:32

1 Make a list of the foods which are **terefah** – forbidden to Jews.

2 Why must Jews buy their meat from a **kosher butcher**?

3 What could be found in **eggs** to make them terefah?

4 What might be in **cheese** to make it terefah?

5 Could Jews eat a cheeseburger made with **kosher meat and kosher cheese**? Give reasons for your answer.

6 Plan a three-course **kosher meal** using both **fish** and **meat** but not in the same course. Include exactly what will be drunk afterwards.

7 Make a list of six foods which are **terefah** and are **eaten regularly by non-Jews**.

8 If you had to equip a **kosher kitchen** write down the basic *extra* things which you would have to buy.

CHAROSET

Before you start, collect your

EQUIPMENT

food processor or liquidizer
mixing bowl
wooden spoon

INGREDIENTS

50g dates, dried or fresh   *½ tsp cayenne pepper*
25g figs   *½ tsp ground ginger*
25g walnuts   *(Kosher for Passover)*
½ tbsp sugar (Kosher for Passover) *1 tbsp sweet red wine (Kosher)*

METHOD

1 Purée the nuts, dates and figs in the food processor.
2 Place in a mixing bowl and stir in the remaining ingredients to make a thick paste.
3 Place in a bowl to serve.

PESACH (PASSOVER) BISCUITS
(see pages 37–39.)

Before you start, set oven at 150°C (Gas Mark 2); collect your

EQUIPMENT

wooden spoon   *baking tray*
grater   *mixing bowl*
fork

INGREDIENTS

150g ground almonds (Kosher)   *75g fine matzah meal*
100g margarine (Kosher)   *(Kosher for Passover)*
100g castor sugar (Kosher)   *1 egg*
                                  1 lemon

METHOD

1 Grease the baking tray.
2 Squeeze the lemon and grate the rind. Beat the egg (remember to check for blood spots).
3 Cream the margarine and sugar together in the mixing bowl.
4 Add the remaining ingredients and mix to a paste.
5 With your hands, roll the mixture into little balls and place on the baking tray.
6 Lightly flatten each ball with the back of a fork.
7 Bake in the oven for 30 minutes.

CHEESECAKE

Before you start,
set oven at 180°C (Gas Mark 4);
collect your

EQUIPMENT

wooden spoon	*20cm loose-bottomed sandwich tin*
electric whisk	*grater*
2 mixing bowls	*pastry board*
rolling pin	*pastry brush*
palette knife	*saucepan*

INGREDIENTS

Pastry

100g self-raising flour	*1 egg yolk*
50g margarine	*vanilla essence (kosher)*
40g icing sugar	

Filling

200g curd cheese	*½ tsp vanilla essence (kosher)*
50g castor sugar	*½ lemon*
25g ground almonds	*2 tbsps currants*
15g margarine	*2 eggs*

Decoration

1 egg white	*granulated sugar*

METHOD

Pastry
1 Grease the sandwich tin.
2 Beat together the icing sugar and margarine in a mixing bowl until smooth.
3 Stir in the remaining ingredients.
4 Turn on to a floured pastry board and roll out.
5 Use three-quarters of the dough to line the tin and put the remainder to one side.

Filling
1 Bring some water to the boil in a saucepan. Drop in the currants and leave for five minutes. Remove from the heat and drain.
2 Separate the 2 eggs (remember to check for blood spots). Squeeze the lemon and grate the rind and place in the mixing bowl.
3 Place all the other ingredients except the egg whites in the bowl and beat together.
4 Beat the 2 egg whites until stiff and fold into the cheese mixture.
5 Spoon the mixture into the pastry case and level with the palette knife.
6 Cut the remaining pastry into strips and lay across the top of the mixture.
7 Beat the remaining egg white until frothy and brush over the pastry.
8 Sprinkle with granulated sugar.
9 Place in the oven and bake for 40 minutes or until golden brown.
10 Remove from the tin and serve while still warm.

TZIMMES

Before you start,
set oven at 190°C (Gas Mark 5);
collect your

EQUIPMENT

frying pan   *chopping board*
chopping knife   *casserole*
mixing bowl   *wooden spoon*
grater

INGREDIENTS

2 medium onions   *1 tsp lemon juice*
2 cloves of garlic   *1 beaten egg (check for blood spots)*
450g carrots   *salt & pepper*
2 tbsp vegetable oil   *3 tbsps ground almonds*
50g medium matzah meal   *¼ tsp ground nutmeg*

METHOD

1 Grease the casserole.
2 Finely chop the onion and garlic. Grate the carrots.
3 Heat the oil in the frying pan and then add the onion and garlic. Fry until golden.
4 Add the carrots to the pan and cook for a further 5 minutes stirring constantly. Remove from the heat.
5 Place the onion, garlic and carrot mixture in the mixing bowl.
6 Add the egg, almonds, lemon juice, salt, pepper and nutmeg to the bowl and mix well.
7 Add the matzah meal and mix together.
8 Place in the greased casserole and bake in the oven for 30 minutes.

POTATO LATKES

Before you start,
collect your

EQUIPMENT

2 large plates	*grater*
metal spoon	*mixing bowl*
fish slice	*frying pan*
fork	*a glass*
plastic bowl	*kitchen paper*

INGREDIENTS

2 large or 4 medium-sized potatoes	*1 clove of garlic*
1 heaped tbsp medium matzah meal	*paprika*
1 small onion	*vegetable cooking oil (for frying)*
1 egg	
salt & pepper to taste	

METHOD

1 Peel the potatoes, onion and garlic. Place in a bowl and cover with water.
2 *Finely* chop the onions and garlic. Grate the potatoes using the large-hole side of the grater.
3 Place the onions, garlic and potatoes in the mixing bowl. Add the matzah meal, salt, pepper and paprika.
4 Break the egg into the glass and check for blood spots. If there are none present, beat it and add to the mixture. Mix thoroughly.
5 Place the oil in the frying pan and heat.
6 When the oil is hot, drop the mixture into the pan, one spoonful at a time.
7 Fry until brown on one side and then turn over until both sides are cooked.
8 Remove from the pan and place on kitchen paper to drain.

JUDAISM WORDSQUARE

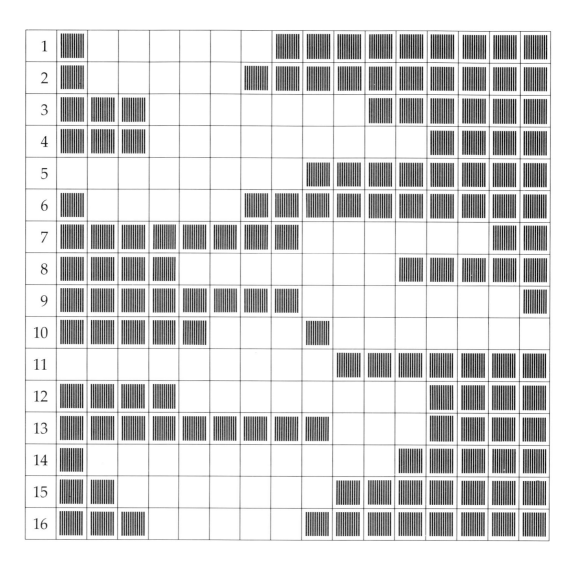

Unravel the words below and write them into the Wordsquare.

1 The Jewish homeland *Ileras*
2 Hear! *amesh*
3 'Nosh' is *ddiishy* for food
4 This is called a shul in number 3 – *gognaysue*
5 There are two of these with thongs – *filletin*
6 The holy scriptures are *oraTh*
7 That's not *rekohs!*
8 You have to do it because it's a *zahmivt*
9 Every door has a *zezumah*
10 For girls only – *zibathvamt*
11 From Eastern Europe come the *izAnekash*
12 … the *fardineS* from the south
13 Number 6 is kept in the *kra*
14 Buy your *kihahanucy* candles in bulk
15 This *puchpah* represents our home
16 Do not go out without your *pelak*

JUDAISM TEST

1 What is the name of the **Jewish homeland**?

2 Who is known as the **Father of Judaism**?

3 What is the Jewish **weekly** holy day called and between what times does it take place?

4 What are the two words for food which Jews:

   a) **can** eat?

   b) **cannot** eat?

5 What is the name of the Jewish **place of public worship**?

6 What is the ceremony called which Jewish boys have when they are thirteen? What is the similar ceremony for girls called?

7 How might you possibly be able to recognize a Jewish man?

8 Why do you think the **scrolls** of the Jewish scriptures are treated with such respect?

9 What is the name of the local **Jewish religious leader**?

10 Why is **Jerusalem** so important to Jews?

JUDAISM ASSESSMENT

1 What is the name of the Jewish **weekly** holy day and what restrictions apply to it?

2 What are the names of the **rites of passage** for a Jewish male?

3 Why are Jewish boys **circumcised**?

4 Why is **Israel** so important to the Jewish people?

5 What place is at the centre of **Jewish worship** and life?

6 Why is the traditional role of the woman so important in Jewish life?

7 Jews are sometimes called **'Children of Abraham and students of Moses'**. Why do you think this is so?

8 What do you see as the advantages and disadvantages of a **ketubah** (marriage contract)?

9 What reasons can you suggest for the speed and simplicity of a Jewish **funeral**?

10 What reason is given for men and women sitting separately in a synagogue?

11 What explanation might be given for **anti-Semitism**?
What would you consider to be the most recent serious incidence of this?

12 What do you understand by the Jewish idea of a **Messiah** and why do Jews and Christians disagree about this?

INTRODUCTION

In many ways *Shabbat*, the Sabbath, is the most important festival of the Jewish calendar and, of course, one which is celebrated at least fifty-two times a year. In Leviticus 23:1–44 the Biblical festivals are listed and the section begins:

The appointed seasons of the LORD, which ye shall proclaim to be holy convocations, even these are MY appointed seasons. Six days shall work be done; but on the seventh day is a sabbath of solemn rest, a holy convocation; ye shall do no manner of work; it is a sabbath unto the LORD in all your dwellings.

The importance of Shabbat in the family and to every Jew cannot be over-stated. In the Talmud it says:

. . . if every Jew kept the Shabbat twice in succession then the Messiah would come.

The festival is celebrated every Friday evening by Jews all over the world.

Note:
The Hebrew word **שבת** is customarily translated as 'Sabbath'. However Jews themselves usually refer to the festival as *Shabbat* (Hebrew) or *Shabbes* (Yiddish).

Stories and Legends
The origin of the Sabbath is in the account of God's Creation of the world in the Torah. The seventh day of the week was when God rested from his work.

And on the seventh day God finished His work which He had made; and He rested on the seventh day from all His work which He had made. And God blessed the seventh day, and hallowed it; because that in it He rested from all His work which God in creating had made.

Genesis 2:2–3

The requirement to keep the Sabbath is found in the Ten Commandments:

Observe the sabbath day, to keep it holy, as the LORD thy God commanded thee. . .

Deuteronomy 5:12

The exact restrictions on what can and cannot be done on the Sabbath are found in the Talmud.

In the Book of Numbers appears the story of the man who gathered sticks on the Sabbath:

And while the children of Israel were in the wilderness, they found a man gathering sticks upon the sabbath day. And they that found him gathering sticks brought him unto Moses and Aaron, and unto all the congregation. And they put him in ward, because it had not been declared what should be done to him. And the LORD said unto Moses: 'The man shall surely be put to death; all the congregation shall stone him with stones without the camp.' And all the congregation brought him without the camp and stoned him with stones, and he died, as the LORD commanded Moses.

Numbers 15:32–36

Legend says that the man gathering sticks is now the Man in the Moon.

Sources
Exodus 20:8–11
Deuteronomy 5:12–15
These books were probably written during the exile in Babylon (c. sixth century B.C.E.). The events referred to took place during the wanderings in Sinai (c. thirteenth century B.C.E.).

Location
The Sabbath is celebrated by services in the synagogue but the principal observance is in the home.

Ritual
The Sabbath day is observed as holy and as a day of rest. The Torah forbids three activities:

. . . let no man go out of his place on the seventh day.

Exodus 16:29

Ye shall kindle no fire throughout your habitations upon the Sabbath day.

Exodus 35:3

. . . in it thou shalt not do any manner of work.

Exodus 20:10

The biblical punishment for breaking the Sabbath is severe:

whosoever doeth any work therein shall be put to death.

Exodus 35:2

There are thirty-nine Sabbath prohibitions divided into seven broad categories. For a listing of these see the Worksheet on Sabbath Laws, p. 32.

In addition there are three other categories added by the Rabbis:

1 *Muktzeh* – objects which are not useable on the Sabbath, such as work tools and money, should not be handled.

2 *Sh'vut* – you should not ask someone to do something on the Sabbath which you cannot do yourself. This does not cover occasions when people are asked to do the act in advance. (Sabbath goys – gentiles who lit fires and turned on lights, etc., on the Sabbath were not instructed on the day itself but beforehand – in the same way they could not be paid on the Sabbath.)

3 *Uvdin d'chol* – weekday things. You should not read business papers, etc.

The Sabbath begins with the lighting of candles in the home by the wife or mother of the family. This ushers in the Sabbath and from then on no work is done. The Sabbath begins eighteen minutes *before* sunset on Friday and ends forty-two minutes *after* sunset on Saturday. This ensures that no work (candle-lighting is work) is done on the Sabbath. Of course the time of sunset varies according to the time of year. These times are now calculated by computer and published in advance (*Judaism in Words and Pictures*, p. 19). However, in the Summer many Jews begin the Sabbath early rather than waiting until ten o'clock to eat. Time may be added to the Sabbath but never subtracted.

The Sabbath meal is very important to Jewish families. It begins with a blessing, *kiddush*, over wine which is then shared. Next, hands are washed. Then two special plaited loaves, *challot* (sing. challah), are blessed and cut. These commemorate the double portion of manna which the Jews received for the Sabbath while they were wandering in the wilderness. Before being cut, the loaves are covered with a cloth called a *decke*. There are three theories regarding this:

1 it represents the dew which fell in the desert.

2 it dresses the challot as a bride dressed for a wedding

> *Shabbat is the Queen in God's kingdom but she is also the Bride of Israel.*
>
> *First Jewish Catalog*

3 the challot are covered so that they do not see the wine being blessed first as they might be offended.

The bread is sprinkled with salt and shared.

Often hymns and songs may be sung during or after the Sabbath meal (*Living Festivals Series – Shabbat*, pp. 8, 10 and 19–21). At the beginning of the Sabbath parents may bless their children;

To a son: *May God make you a symbol of blessing as He did Ephraim and Manasseh.*

To a daughter: *May God make you a symbol of blessing as He did Sarah, Rebekah, Rachel and Leah.*

Husbands may praise their wives at this time by reciting Proverbs 31.

Because no work can be done, all meals have to be prepared in advance. Large urns are filled with water and heated, and slow-cooking food is placed in the oven in advance. Ashkenazi Jews call this type of casserole *cholent* and Sefardi Jews call it *adfina* or *chamin*. Modern ovens with electric timers have made this cooking in advance much easier.

In a real emergency such as a medical condition, Sabbath rules are lifted in order to save life.

There are services for the Sabbath in the synagogue on Friday and Saturday. Generally the morning service follows this form:

1 Morning blessings of thanksgiving.
2 Blessings and psalms ending with the Song of Moses (Exodus 15:1–18).
3 The Shema.
4 *Amidah* or standing prayer.
5 Torah service – the scrolls are carried around the syngagogue and the week's portion of the Torah is read. This is followed by a reading from the Prophets, the *haftarah* – completion.
6 *Musaf* – additional service for the Sabbath.
7 *Aleynu* – praises to God; then psalms and hymns.
8 *Kiddush* – the congregation say blessings over wine and challot again.

The Sabbath concludes with the *Havdalah* service. This marks the end of the day. A plaited candle is lit and a blessing is said over a cup of wine. Then a spice box is passed around so that the sweetness of the Sabbath may remain with everyone for the following week. A blessing is said over the candle flame. Then follows this prayer:

Blessed art thou, O Lord our God, King of the universe, who makest a distinction between holy and profane, between light and darkness, between Israel and other nations, between the seventh day and the six working days. Blessed art thou, O Lord, who makest a distinction between holy and profane.

Siddur

A few drops of wine are poured into a dish and the candle is extinguished in them. The wine is passed around and people greet each other with *Shavuah Tov* – a good week. (In Yiddish, a *gute voch*.)

Artefacts

Sabbath candles and candlesticks, Kiddush cup, wine, challot, challah knife (this must be a special knife – an ordinary one would imply work), havdalah candle, havdalah spice box.

Food

Wine and challot are fundamental to the Sabbath but other foods are also traditional: chicken, gefilte fish, parve cake or fruit salad. For Saturday the traditional food is cholent (or adfina) with kugel or rice.

Significant Persons

The family and the Rabbi. Historically the festival was instituted by God and announced to the people by Moses.

THEMES FOR THE CLASSROOM

1 The Sabbath and the family are at the centre of Jewish life and worship. The specialness of the day should be considered along with the great preparations which are made in order that it can be kept properly. The welcoming in of the Sabbath bride is important as is the very special role of women in this festival. It is also important to see the Havdalah as marking the end of the Sabbath; the return to normal weekday life.

2 Non-Jewish pupils can be asked to think how it would change their lives if they were to celebrate a day in this way every week.

3 The way in which God provided for the Israelites in the wilderness can be considered here; in particular the manna and the double portion for the Sabbath.

4 The problems which Jews living in a non-Jewish society may have in particular with regard to eating and celebrating festivals can be considered in work on the Sabbath.

5 The way in which the whole family is involved in the celebration; the sharing of the wine and challot and the blessings given to them.

6 The Sabbath morning service in the synagogue can be utilized as an introduction to Jewish prayer and communal worship.

7 Teachers might explore the idea that a commandment such as that to keep the Sabbath, made over 3000 years ago, is still adhered to today despite all the changes in life which have taken place since then. The importance which Jews attach to God's word and his wishes.

THE WORKSHEETS

The first worksheet is based on the Sabbath laws. The second is on the structure of the synagogue.

These are followed by a Wordsearch on Shabbat and finally by a test and full assessment.

SHABBAT LAWS

Here is a list of things which **cannot** be done on the Sabbath. Look at it very carefully.

1 Growing and preparing food

Ploughing	Sowing	Reaping
Stacking sheaves	Threshing	Winnowing
Selecting out	Sifting	Grinding
Kneading	Cooking	

2 Making clothing

Sheep shearing	Washing	Combining raw
Dyeing	Spinning	materials
Weaving	Removing a	Threading a loom
Separating threads	finished article	Untying knots
Sewing	Tying knots	Tearing

3 Leatherwork and writing

Trapping	Slaughtering	Flaying skins
Tanning	Scraping	Marking out
Cutting	Writing	Erasing

4 Providing shelter

Building	Demolishing

5 Creating fire

Kindling a fire	Extinguishing a fire

6 Work completion
Completing an object or making it useable

7 Transporting goods
Carrying in a public place

In addition there are three other groups:

1 **Muktzeh** – objects which are not useable on the Sabbath, such as work tools and money, should not be handled.

2 **Sh'vut** – you should not ask someone else to do something on the Sabbath which you cannot do yourself unless you ask them in advance.

3 **Uvdin d'chol** – weekday things. You should not read business papers, etc.

Think about everything which a non-Jewish person might do from sunset on Friday until an hour after sunset on Saturday. Make a list and then mark those activities which a Jew could **not** undertake during this time.

THE SYNAGOGUE

Here is an outline plan of a typical Orthodox synagogue. Mark these objects on the plan:

1 compass points

2 Ner Tamid – the everlasting light

3 Bimah – where the scrolls are read

4 Parochet – curtain

5 Menorah

6 Holy Ark

7 Seats for the men

8 Gallery for the women

9 Lectern for the chazzan

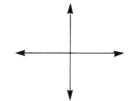

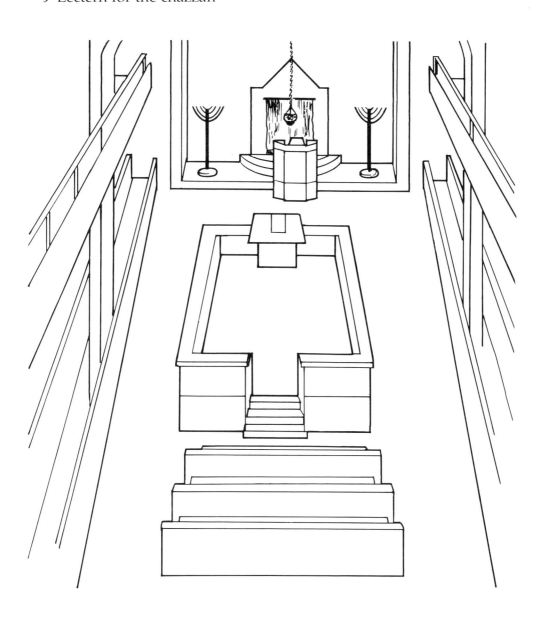

SHABBAT WORDSEARCH

L	H	S	H	A	L	A	D	V	A	H	U	N	E	L	A	P
E	A	N	L	O	H	C	D	N	I	D	R	U	K	C	T	E
H	R	R	O	S	H	A	B	B	A	T	U	L	C	H	X	D
C	O	U	E	M	A	N	A	S	S	E	H	O	E	O	O	T
A	T	V	B	U	M	B	W	O	R	K	E	N	D	L	B	M
R	E	S	T	Y	U	O	B	A	D	F	I	N	A	E	E	U
N	T	R	M	O	S	E	S	A	V	W	X	D	O	N	C	K
S	D	E	T	I	A	L	P	H	T	H	U	R	D	T	I	T
E	G	B	S	A	F	O	R	T	A	E	A	U	X	U	P	Z
B	E	E	H	N	I	A	N	I	S	B	P	E	J	V	S	E
B	F	K	E	A	U	E	S	F	B	H	B	H	L	H	U	H
A	I	A	M	D	E	S	R	I	K	A	Z	E	R	S	Q	U
H	L	H	A	I	E	I	O	H	A	R	A	S	S	A	C	Y
S	T	N	E	M	D	N	A	M	M	O	C	N	E	T	I	L
O	E	C	H	A	L	L	O	T	E	T	L	E	G	U	K	M
P	A	E	Y	A	D	R	U	T	A	S	E	L	D	N	A	C

RABBI	URDIN D'CHOL	WINE
SHABBAT	SHABBES	SPICE BOX
PLAITED	CANDLES	MUSAF
WORK	KUGEL	REBEKAH
FRIDAY	SATURDAY	CHOLENT
HAVDALAH	MANASSEH	SHEMA
CHALLOT	ADFINA	SEVEN
URNS	RACHEL	REST
EPHRAIM	SINAI	KIDDUSH
LEAH	MESSIAH	DECKE
SHVUT	TORAH	GEFILTE
MOSES	TEN COMMANDMENTS	AMIDA
SABBATH	SUNSET	SARAH
		MUKTZEH

SHABBAT TEST

1 What part of the Bible tells the Jews to keep the **Sabbath**?

2 What was the original punishment for not keeping the Sabbath?

3 In what 2 places do Jews celebrate the Sabbath?

4 How does a woman **'bring in'** the Sabbath?

5 What are **challot**?

6 How long does the Sabbath last?

7 What can Jews not do on the Sabbath? Give 5 examples.

8 What is the special name for the type of **foods** which Jews may eat at lunch-time on the Sabbath?

9 What is the name of the **service** which ends the Sabbath?

10 Why is this day so important to Jews?

SHABBAT ASSESSMENT

1 Why is the **Sabbath** so important to Jews?

2 What is the particular importance of women in the celebration of the Sabbath?

3 What preparations need to be made in advance of the Sabbath?

4 Shabbat is sometimes called the **'Queen of Festivals'** – can you suggest why?

5 Describe a Sabbath **morning service** in the syngagogue.

6 What is the importance of passing around the **spice box** at the Havdalah service?

7 **Challot** have a special importance. What do they represent?

8 Describe how Jews in England managed their lights and fires on the Sabbath before the introduction of central heating, electric timers, etc.

9 Why are candles lit eighteen minutes *before* sunset?

10 What special features of the Jewish way of life may have caused the Sabbath to be celebrated almost unchanged for thousands of years?

11 What difficulties do you think **Diaspora Jews** might experience in celebrating the Sabbath?

12 Jews attach special importance to food and say many blessings over it – why do you think this is so?

Passover

INTRODUCTION

The festival of *Pesach* or Passover marks the beginning of the religious year and is celebrated from 15 Nisan to 22 Nisan. The first and last days of the festival are days of rest when no work, apart from preparing food, should be done. If they fall on the Sabbath then food must of course be prepared in advance.

Passover celebrates the night when the Angel of Death passed over (pesach) the houses of the Israelites in Egypt but killed the first-born of the Egyptians. It is also the first pilgrim festival of the year, celebrating the barley harvest.

Its importance is such that it must be celebrated by every Jew as though they themselves had come out of Egypt.

In the Torah it is referred to as *Chag Hamatzot*, the feast of unleavened bread. The Jews at the first Passover ate *matzot* (sing. matzah) – hard dry rough bread without yeast, not the rich bread of free people. Matzot are also *lechem cherut* – the bread of freedom.

Seven days shall ye eat unleavened bread; howbeit the first day ye shall put away leaven out of your houses; for whosoever eateth leavened bread from the first day until the seventh day, that soul shall be cut off from Israel.

Seven days shall there be no leaven found in your houses; for whosoever eateth that which is leavened, that soul shall be cut off from the congregation of Israel ...

Exodus 12:15 and 19

Chametz is not the five grains – wheat, rye, barley, oats and spelt (a type of wheat). It is the leavened product when any of these come into contact with water for more than eighteen minutes. Matzot are permitted because it is carefully watched to ensure that no water touches the flour before it is ready for preparation and then for no more than eighteen minutes before baking.

This is as far as the restrictions apply to Sefardim, but the Ashkenazim cannot eat rice, corn, beans, peas and peanuts.

All food must be checked for chametz. It is removed from the house in two ways:

1 *biur* – burning – the destruction of the food – every room in the house is cleaned for crumbs in this way and toothbrushes, etc., are replaced.

2 *bitul* – renouncing – by the procedure of *mechirat chametz* – it is sold to a non-Jew for the period of the festival and then bought back again – the important thing being that it does not remain in the possession of the household.

Even the slightest trace of chametz must be removed. During the rest of the year the laws of kashrut allow up to one part in sixty of non-kosher food without it affecting the remainder, but at Passover *all* chametz must be removed.

Special food is bought for Passover and is labelled *Kosher for Passover* or *Kosher for Pesach* with the stamp on it of a rabbinical authority. This includes many food items, such as matzot and matzah meal (ground matzot used instead of flour), baking powder, some spices, jams and margarine.

The whole of the kitchen and home must be *pesachdik* – fit for Passover. Many people have special sets of crockery and utensils for use at Passover which are kept locked away for the rest of the year. In addition, all articles which remain and need to be used for food preparation are kashered. The means of doing this depends on how the object can absorb the chametz; therefore some objects are soaked, others heated.

There are five Sabbaths leading up to Passover with special Torah readings:

Shabbat Shekalim	– the duty to give a shekel to the Temple.
Shabbat Zachor	– the Sabbath of remembrance – remember how the Jews were treated by Haman (see Purim, page 85).
Shabbat Parah	– the Sabbath of purification – Jews should purify themselves before purifying the house for Passover.
Shabbat Hachodesh	– 'the month' – regulations for Passover.
Shabbat Hagadol	– the Great Sabbath – the day on which the Israelites sprinkled blood on their doorposts to ward off the Angel of Death.

Maot Chittin – money for wheat – this collection is made to ensure that everyone can celebrate Passover.

Erev Pesach On the night before Passover the house is searched by candlelight (usually by a child) to find any remaining chametz. Often the mother will have hidden a few pieces to be found. The most common numbers of pieces is ten; it is easy to remember and can be associated with the Ten Commandments and the Ten Plagues.

The pieces are collected into a bag and their ownership is renounced. The prayer, *Kol Chamira*, is in Aramaic:

All leaven and all chametz which is in my possession, which I have not seen or destroyed, nor have knowledge of shall be null, void, ownerless, and as dust of the earth.

Haggadah

This covers all eventualities of having missed or forgotten something.

The following morning the last meal of chametz is eaten and by the time one third of daylight is over, the remaining food is burnt and the Kol Chamira is repeated.

Fast of the first-born – in thanksgiving for the life of the first-born of the Israelites, it is a tradition that the first-born son of each family should fast on Erev Pesach. In order to avoid this, a custom arose of finishing the reading of a tract of the Talmud on this day so that a *siyyum* can be celebrated. This is a celebration when Kiddush is said as a mitzvah. Once this is done the fast does not have to be kept.

The Seder – the details of the Seder meal and the reading of the Haggadah are included in *Living Festivals – Passover*. However, a point which needs to be made is that half-way through the Seder an instruction in the Haggadah says:

The Table is Set.

At this point everyone shares the festival meal before the completion of the reading of the Haggadah.

The whole meal, the glasses of wine, the pillows for reclining and the Seder meal serve as a teaching aid; a reminder of slavery and how the Jews were freed, and the life of freedom that they lived thereafter.

The Seder is in fourteen sections:

Kadesh	– blessing over the wine
U'rechatz	– washing the hands
Karpas	– eating the karpas
Yachatz	– dividing the matzah
Maggid	– telling the Passover story
Rachtzah	– washing the hands
Motzi matzah	– blessings over the matzah
Maror	– eating the bitter herbs
Korech	– the sandwich
Shulchan Orech	– the festival meal
Tzafun	– eating the afikoman
Barech	– grace after meals
Hallel	– Hallel
Nirtzah	– conclusion

The meal ends with everyone saying:

'*L'Shana Ha'ba'ah Be'Yerushalayim*' – 'Next Year in Jerusalem'.

(In Israel itself this is changed to: '*Next Year in Jerusalem, rebuilt*'.)

The Second Seder – in the Diaspora the Seder meal is repeated on the second night.

The prayers in the synagogue change at this time and the prayer for rain which has been said since Simchat Torah is replaced by the prayer for dew, and God is asked to bless the earth rather than to bring rain.

Starting with the second night of Passover the *Counting of the Omer* begins (see Shavuot, page 48).

Artefacts

Seder plate, Passover crockery and cutlery, Haggadah, pillows and cup for Elijah.

Food

From the beginning of Passover all food that is used must be 'Kosher for Passover'. Flour is not permitted but matzah meal is (see page 37).

The special Seder meal which is eaten at Passover contains several ritual items:

זרוע **zeroa** a lamb shankbone

ביצה **beytza** a roasted egg

כרפס **karpas** a spring vegetable

מרור **maror** bitter herbs

Each of these represents some aspect of the Israelites' escape:

zeroa	the Passover sacrifice and also *Zecher L'churban* – the destruction of the Temple. Also in memory of the Egyptians who died. Zeroa means arm, God's arm outstretched to deliver the Israelites.
beytza	*Korban Chagigah*, the Temple sacrifice that can no longer be offered.
karpas	Spring and new life.
maror	the bitterness endured by the slaves.

There is also the sweet-tasting **חרוסת**, Charoset, which represents the mortar which the slaves used in labouring for the Egyptians, and bowls of salt water for the tears of the Israelites.

In Ashkenazi homes the festival meal usually begins with hard-boiled eggs dipped in salt water: eggs are a sign of Spring, of renewal and new life; the salt water is the tears of the slaves and also tears for the dead Egyptians. The meal itself will often be chicken soup and matzah balls followed by a casserole of some kind. There is a custom of not eating roast meat because of its similarity to the lamb which can no longer be sacrificed since the loss of the Temple.

Significant Persons

Moses, Pharoah, the Israelites.

THEMES FOR THE CLASSROOM

Passover in particular has been studied in schools for so long that we need to think of new themes and ways of introducing it to pupils. However, because of its great importance in Jewish life and the special importance of the Seder itself, there are some points which do need to be considered.

1 The Seder meal is part of religious worship. It has become fashionable to re-enact the meal in classrooms with readings from the Haggadah. This must be a very questionable activity. Many religions are now studied in schools but whereas there can be little objection to the acting out of stories associated with religious belief such as that of Rama and Sita or indeed of Esther, the idea of 'staging' a Seder is totally different. One presumes that neither teachers nor parents would like the idea of all children or indeed any non-Muslim children being asked to perform wudu and Muslim prayer. It seems unlikely that people would like the idea of children 'consecrating' and 'administering' the Christian Eucharist. Why then is it seen as not only all right but indeed good educational practice to act out a Seder?

As well as being illogical there are the following particular reasons for not doing this:

(a) – The Seder is a religious event not just story-telling.
(b) – food which is not prepared by a Jew in a kosher kitchen is not edible by Jews. Therefore a school Seder cannot be partaken of by the people who, in reality, celebrate it.

(c) – a Seder prepared outside Passover even given the restrictions above is not a Seder because the food is not 'Kosher for Passover'.

(The fact that Jews invite Gentiles to share the meal with them is a totally different discussion.)

2 The symbolic use made of food during this festival and the complex preparations should be considered. To this can be allied the use made of food in other faiths and the importance which we attach to food.

3 God's love for the people who love him and the way in which he acts to save the Israelites. Perhaps the simplicity of this needs to be contrasted for the older pupils with the Holocaust.

4 One of the most interesting ideas is that even in this night of rejoicing there is always a sadness. While rejoicing in their own freedom the Jews spill wine because of the dead Egyptians. While celebrating they still hope to return to Jerusalem rebuilt.

5 The Torah is the complete revelation of God's will. On the other hand, however, the Haggadah is a marvellous example of the collecting together of ideas of wisdom and learning to continue its explanation.

THE WORKSHEETS

The first worksheet is to design a Seder plate. The next is a poster based on the Plagues of Egypt.

There is a piece of Home Economics work on chametz and then a chance to compose new music for a traditional Passover song.

Finally there is a Wordsquare and Wordsearch on Passover and a test and full assessment.

THE SEDER PLATE

On page 21 of the *Living Festivals – Passover* book, you will find a picture of a Seder plate. On this page is the outline of a plate. Using the outline draw and decorate a plate of your own. Include the names of the foods which go on it in both Hebrew and English. You can also draw pictures of them on the plate. Underneath each food write down what it represents.

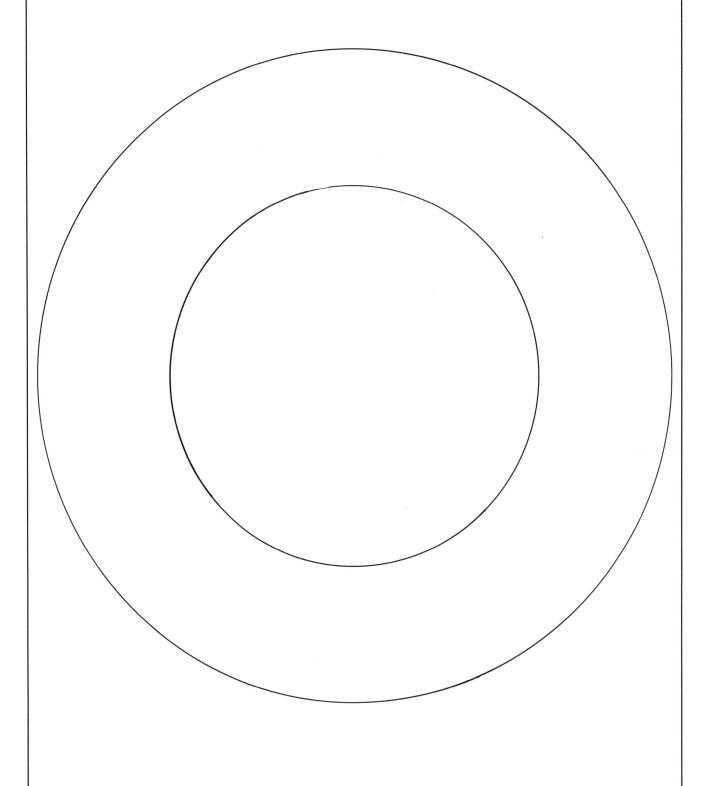

THE PLAGUES OF EGYPT

In **Exodus, Chapters 7–11** are the Ten Plagues of Egypt.

Blood

Frogs

Lice

Flies

Blight

Boils

Hail

Locusts

Darkness

Death of the First-born

Make a warning poster for the Egyptians illustrating each of the plagues and showing what will happen unless they allow the Israelites to go.

FREE OF CHAMETZ

This page shows a list of some foods which are approved as being *Kosher for Passover*.

Chose fifteen of them. Check other brands and similar foods and find out what they contain which makes them non-Kosher for Passover.

Grodzinski	**Chocolate Gateau**
Snowcrest	**Crisps**
Snowcrest	**Cottage Cheese**
W & F Fish Products	**Smoked Salmon**
Snowcrest	**Lemon Sorbet**
Assis	**Orange Juice**
Snowcrest	**Marmalade**
Rowse	**Honey**
Snowcrest	**Raspberry Jelly**
Carmel	**Potato Latkes**
Rakusens	**Soft Tub Margarine**
Unigate	**Milk**
Maydew	**Ground Almonds**
Simons	**Table Salt**
Barons	**Salad Cream**
Snowcrest	**Lemon Drink**
Hebrew National	**Tomato Soup (parev)**
Tate & Lyle	**Granulated Sugar**
Ridgeways	**Tea Bags**
Gilberts	**Chopped Liver**
Gilberts	**Beef Sausages**
Kelmans	**Beef Burgers**
Country Life	**English Butter**
Selecta	**Cheddar Cheese**
Elite	**Milk Chocolate**
Haddar	**Tinned Pineapple**
Haddar	**Tomato Ketchup**
Osem	**Mushroom Soup**
Selecta	**Instant Coffee**
Golden Rose	**Cooking Fat**
Herczl	**Double Cream**
Haddar	**Tinned Sardines**
Bar Fenura	**Asti Spumante – Sparkling Wine**
Rumplers	**Barley Sugar**

PASSOVER SONGS

Below are the words of a traditional Passover song.

Write some music for the song which you and your class can sing and perform. It must have a strong rhythm for everyone to clap along to.

Passover Song

One who knows? One I know: One is our God that is in Heaven and Earth.

Two who knows? Two I know: Two are the Tables of the Law, One …

Three who knows? Three I know: Three are the Patriarch Fathers, Two …, One …

Four are the Mothers of Israel

Five are the Books of the Torah

Six are the Divisions of the Mishnah

Seven are the days of the week

At eight days a boy is circumcised

At nine months a child is born

Ten are the Commandments

Eleven stars did Joseph see

Twelve are the Tribes of Israel

Thirteen are the attributes of God

PASSOVER WORDSQUARE

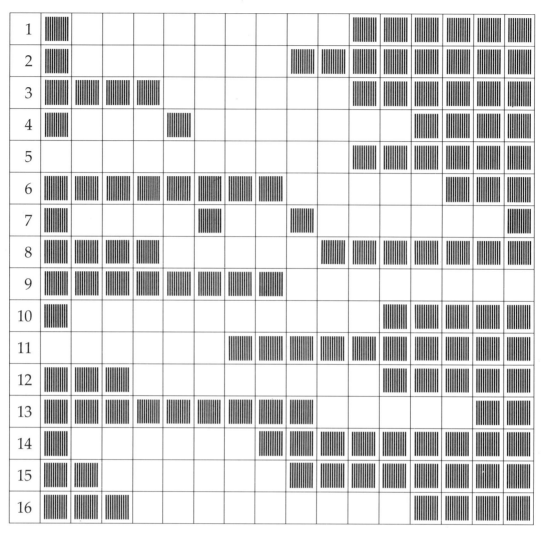

1 At Passover the house must be P_____
2 by removing all the C_____
3 this is all the L_____
4 Pesach marks the last of the T_____ P_____
5 when the I_____
6 finally left E_____
7 This story appears in the B_____ ____ E_____
8 It is retold each year at the S_____ meal
9 when it is read from the H_____
10 During this meal people eat U_____ bread
11 called M_____
12 They also eat the sweet-tasting C_____
13 bitter herbs called M_____
14 and K_____ which are green vegetables
15 A cup of wine is poured for the Prophet E_____
16 At the end of the meal people say that next year they hope to eat it in
  J_____

PASSOVER WORDSEARCH

E	A	S	T	U	R	E	H	C	M	E	H	C	E	L	L	K
N	O	A	M	S	T	U	N	A	E	P	O	T	L	A	S	A
I	Z	P	U	J	H	I	A	M	L	P	O	B	E	A	N	S
W	T	R	Y	P	A	S	S	O	V	E	R	W	A	S	T	H
M	E	A	Y	O	J	R	I	R	E	S	T	O	V	E	A	R
A	M	K	I	S	I	A	N	T	B	A	R	L	E	Y	Z	U
O	A	T	S	S	L	E	B	A	I	C	V	L	N	R	T	T
T	H	Y	N	R	E	L	Y	R	U	H	S	I	V	D	Y	E
C	C	T	I	D	S	I	A	O	R	E	Z	P	E	W	E	A
H	H	C	A	M	A	T	Z	O	T	R	L	U	T	I	B	R
I	E	O	N	W	H	E	A	T	U	I	S	P	E	L	T	S
T	R	X	R	O	K	S	E	D	E	R	Y	A	S	G	G	E
T	B	T	O	Z	T	A	M	A	H	G	A	H	C	F	E	P
I	S	E	C	D	S	A	E	P	E	R	O	R	A	M	E	T
N	P	L	A	G	U	E	S	H	A	D	A	G	G	A	H	P
R	V	E	W	P	E	S	A	C	H	D	I	K	S	T	E	R

PASSOVER	CHAMETZ	HERBS
BARLEY	OATS	MORTAR
LECHEM CHERUT	CORN	BITUL
TEARS	EGGS	SIYYUM
RYE	MAROR	ISRAELITES
RICE	BIUR	EXODUS
PEANUTS	MAOT CHITTIN	PLAGUES
KARPAS	SALT	WHEAT
ZEROA	NISAN	SPELT
PESACHDIK	CHAG HAMATZOT	PEAS
WINE	HAGGADAH	PILLOW
PESACH	LEAVEN	BEYTZA
MATZOT	SEDER	KASHRUT
EGYPT	BEANS	ELIJAH

PASSOVER TEST

1 Sort out the following words which are connected with Passover

chapes   tomzat   stielesria   gulpaes

mechatz   reeds   pygte   rifts-bron

semos   dhagagah

2 What is *leaven*?

3 Why must all food containing leaven be **sold or destroyed** before Passover?

4 What foods are on a **Seder plate**?

5 Who is the **special guest** who is hoped for at each Seder meal?

6 At the end of the meal Jews say: **'Next year in Jerusalem'**. Why do you think they do this?

7 Why is a drop of wine **spilled** at the mention of each plague?

8 What food is used instead of **flour** during Passover?

9 What does **charoset** represent?

10 Imagine that you have been to a **Seder meal**. Write a letter describing it to a friend.

PASSOVER ASSESSMENT

1 When does **Passover** take place?

2 If people know only one **Jewish festival** it will probably be **Passover**. Why do you think this is so?

3 What are the **FIVE items** on a **Seder plate** and what do they represent?

4 Why is **roast meat** traditionally *not* eaten at a Seder meal?

5 What is special about the technique used for baking **matzot for Passover**?

6 What is the **reason for Passover** and many other festivals being celebrated for **a day longer** in the Diaspora than in Israel?

7 What is the importance of the **pillows** at the Seder meal?

8 What is the **Haggadah**? What does the word mean and what does the book contain?

9 Detail the **preparations** made for Passover in the home. What part do children play in this?

10 One **prayer** is said at this time which is *not* in Hebrew. What language is it in and what is the prayer about?

11 Why is Passover both a **sad and a happy occasion**? Give as many reasons as you can for this.

12 Explain the reason for the **absence of leaven** in the house at this time.

Shavuot

INTRODUCTION

Shavuot – the Feast of Weeks (in Greek, *Pentecost*) takes place on 6 Sivan. It is the least known of all the major Jewish festivals. It is the second pilgrim festival of the year. Jews travelled from as far away as Egypt, Italy, Greece and Babylon in order to fulfil the mitzvah that the first fruits of the wheat harvest, represented by two loaves, should be brought to the Temple in Jerusalem.

Shavuot has many names. The Torah calls the festival *Chag Habikkurim* – the festival of the first fruits.

In the *Siddur* – prayer book – the festival is called 'The Season of the Giving of our Torah'. It remembers the giving of the Torah and specifically the receiving by Moses of the Ten Commandments on Mount Sinai.

The festival is sometimes called *Atseret*, which means 'stop' – perhaps because there was little ritual associated with the day apart from stopping work.

The name *Atseret shel Pesach* – 'Conclusion of Passover' – refers to the end of the season of harvests which began at Passover with barley. Also the freedom from slavery at Passover was not made whole until the Jews received the Torah.

The period from Passover to Shavuot is called *Sefirat Omer* – 'the counting of Omer'. An *Omer* is a measure of barley. One Omer was brought to the Temple in Jerusalem every night for fifty nights beginning on the second day of Passover. This is commanded in Leviticus 23:15 and the word Pentecost is derived from the Greek word for 'fiftieth'.

From this it can be seen that there are two different ideas associated with Shavuot: the harvest and the giving of the Torah. The shift from the one to the other probably happened during the first century C.E. after the destruction of the Temple.

The three days preceding Shavuot are described in the Torah as special days when Jews should purify themselves ready to receive the Torah. These are called *Sheloshet Yemai Hagbalah*. They are no longer formally observed.

Stories and Legends

The two principal stories associated with Shavuot are the giving of the Torah and the story of Ruth.

Legend says that King David was born and died on Shavuot. It is also said that on the night of Shavuot the heavens open to receive prayers and study.

Sources

Leviticus 23:15–21.
The date is about 1250 B.C.E..

TIKKUN LEYL SHAVUOT
This is a special book of religious literature devised for studying on the night of Shavuot: it contains selections from the written and oral law with between three and seven verses from the beginning and end of each part of the Torah with some sections read complete. The Torah readings are followed by the 63 treatises of the *Mishnah* and the 613 mitzvot of *Maimonides*.

Location

The festival is celebrated in the synagogue and at home. The origins of the festival lie:
a) in the Temple in Jerusalem for the harvest festival.
b) in the wilderness of Sinai for the giving of the Torah.

Ritual

In memory of the original sacrifice, two long challot are used in the home.

As well as the sacrifice of the first fruits of the grain harvest, other observances are associated with Shavuot:

1 The Book of Ruth is read in the synagogue.
2 Dairy foods are eaten at the festival as the Torah is like milk and honey (Song of Songs 4:11). Also, until the revelation on Mount Sinai the laws about kosher food were not given and therefore meat and fish were avoided.
3 The home and the synagogue are decorated with greenery and flowers. This is a reminder that the slopes of Mount Sinai were covered with vegetation in honour of the Torah.

Synagogue readings are:

Exodus 19 and 20 – giving of the Ten Commandments.
Ezekiel 1 – visions of God.
Habakkuk 3 – God's power in revelation.

48

Ruth – this mentions harvest, the gleaners and deals with a Moabite woman who marries an Israelite but whose attachment to his family and beliefs continues after his death. (Leviticus 23:22 orders the Israelites to leave some of their crop ungathered for the poor to glean.)

4 The entire night of Shauvot is spent studying the Torah. This is an attempt to be awake to the revelations of God because the Israelites fell asleep while waiting for Moses to come down from Mount Sinai. Some people study Tikkun leyl Shavuot at this time.

5 Shavuot is about learning and education and at one time it was the occasion on which children were first taken to Hebrew classes.

6 There is a special Sefardi tradition associated with Shavuot. After the Ark is opened in the morning a ketubah (marriage contract) is read between God (the groom) and Israel (the bride). The groom's wedding gift to his bride is the Torah and the oral law.

Artefacts
Long Shavuot challot. Flowers and greenery. The scroll of Ruth.

Food
Dairy foods – milche. Cheesecake and blintzes are especially eaten at this time. Another food is cheese kreplach – this three-sided pastry is said to represent the giving of Torah in three sections – Torah, Prophets, Writings; to three peoples – Cohen, Levite, Israelite; to a third-born child – Moses; in the third month, Sivan.

Significant Persons
Moses, Ruth, David, children.

THEMES FOR THE CLASSROOM

There are three important themes associated with Shavuot which can be explored in the classroom:

1 Harvest and the duty to give thanks by bringing offerings of the harvested food to God.

2 The giving of the Torah and especially of the Ten Commandments – the great gift which God bestowed on the Israelites. Here there is an opportunity within festivals work to look at the Ten Commandments and to consider their importance. The eating of dairy foods because the Torah is 'milk and honey' demonstrates the value placed on it by the Jewish people. This importance is also stressed by the practice of sitting up all night to study the Law. The importance of studying the Torah and of education itself is shown by the sending of young children to *cheder* (Hebrew School) for the first time at this festival.

3 Shavuot is seen as the conclusion of Passover and pupils might consider the idea that the Jews were not really freed from their slavery until they received the gift of the truth of the Torah.

THE WORKSHEETS

The first worksheet is an opportunity to consider the modern implications of the Ten Commandments. This is followed by a simple retelling of the story of Ruth.

There is a Wordsearch on Shavuot and finally a test and full assessment.

THE TEN COMMANDMENTS

Here are the Ten Commandments as they appear in the book of **Exodus:**

> I am the LORD thy God
> You shall have no other gods before me. You shall not make any graven image
> You shall not take the name of the LORD your God in vain
> Remember the Sabbath day and keep it holy
> Honour your father and mother
> You shall not murder
> You shall not commit adultery
> You shall not steal
> You shall not bear false witness
> You shall not covet

1 Think carefully about these and then, in your own words, write down how far you believe these apply to life today. Then, write them out in more modern English as a model for people to live by.

2 Now, read this poem by the Victorian poet Clough. It is called *The Latest Decalogue*:

> *Thou shalt have one God Only; who*
> *Would be at the expense of two?*
> *No graven images may be*
> *Worshipped, except the currency:*
> *Swear not at all; for for thy curse*
> *Thine enemy is none the worse:*
> *At church on Sunday to attend*
> *Will serve to keep the world thy friend:*
> *Honour thy parents; that is, all*
> *From whom advancement may befall:*
> *Thou shalt not kill; but needst not strive*
> *Officiously to keep alive:*
> *Do not adultery commit;*
> *Advantage rarely comes of it:*
> *Thou shalt not steal; an empty feat,*
> *When it's so lucrative to cheat:*
> *Bear not false witness; let the lie*
> *Have time on its own wings to fly:*
> *Thou shalt not covet; but tradition*
> *Approves all forms of competition.*

3 In your opinion which version of the Ten Commandments most accurately shows how most people live today? Taking each commandment in turn, write down your explanation of the Clough poem and suggest why some people tend to live more like this suggests than as the Bible tells them to.

THE STORY OF RUTH

Read the following story which is taken from the Book of Ruth in the Bible. You will notice that the sentences are not in the right order. Sort them into the correct order and then write them out on a large sheet of paper drawing pictures to illustrate the story as well.

Ten years later Naomi's sons both died and she decided to go back to her own people.

On the way Naomi told them that they should return to their own mothers but they refused.

Eventually they were married and had a son called Obed.

She said that Naomi's people would be hers and that Naomi's God would be hers.

Ruth was not an Israelite but a young woman from the land of Moab.

When they reached Israel Ruth worked in the fields gathering the barley that was left over after the harvesters had finished.

Naomi told them again to return and this time Orpah went back but Ruth stayed.

Ruth and Orpah decided to go with her.

Ruth continued on the journey with Naomi and said that she would go with her and live with her.

Soon Boaz knew all about Ruth and the way in which she had looked after Naomi.

Ruth and another girl called Orpah married the two sons of an Israelite widow called Naomi who had come to Moab with her husband.

She worked in the fields of a man called Boaz.

Obed was to be the grandfather of King David.

SHAVUOT WORDSEARCH

T	O	U	V	A	H	S	L	Y	E	L	N	U	K	K	I	T
P	F	O	K	L	S	G	N	O	S	F	O	G	N	O	S	E
I	R	L	E	V	I	T	I	C	U	S	I	N	A	I	G	R
L	U	B	T	A	T	O	U	V	A	H	S	R	E	T	U	E
G	I	A	U	T	O	V	Z	T	I	M	K	L	P	A	S	M
R	T	R	B	T	S	O	L	E	T	N	E	P	O	L	D	O
I	S	L	A	W	E	H	H	U	E	A	E	I	T	Y	B	T
M	D	E	H	G	I	A	A	X	R	E	W	G	S	F	N	A
S	H	Y	V	I	O	R	N	J	E	L	S	R	U	T	H	R
W	E	E	D	A	R	O	H	C	S	G	F	I	F	T	Y	I
C	D	H	A	R	O	T	S	R	T	N	M	M	U	I	O	F
E	C	E	E	R	G	L	I	B	A	S	U	T	P	Y	G	E
B	A	B	Y	L	O	N	M	A	I	M	O	N	I	D	E	S
E	D	C	H	A	G	H	A	B	I	K	K	U	R	I	M	L
A	S	D	A	V	I	D	R	A	F	E	S	S	I	V	A	N
C	H	E	E	S	E	C	A	K	E	U	L	E	A	R	S	I

SHAVUOT	RUTH	ITALY
WHEAT	STOP	SINAI
CHAG HABIKKURIM	BABYLON	PILGRIM
KETUBAH	MISHNAH	ATSERET
TORAH	CHEESECAKE	SEFIRAT OMER
GREECE	TIKKUN LEYL SHAVUOT	MITZVOT
ISRAEL	PENTECOST	EGYPT
MAIMONIDES	LOAVES	DAVID
SIVAN	FIFTY	LEVITICUS
WEEKS	SEFARDI	SONG OF SONGS
GLEAN	FRUITS	

SHAVUOT TEST

1 Give **TWO other names** for this festival.

2 Shavuot is a **harvest festival**. What was being harvested at this time?

3 Where did **Moses** receive the **Ten Commandments**?

4 Why do people often eat **dairy foods** at this festival?

5 What **special book** of the Bible is read at Shavuot?

6 People sometimes **sit up all night** at Shavuot. What do they do?

7 What reason is given for **decorating homes and synagogues** with plants and flowers for Shavuot?

8 Why is the **number 50** so important at this festival?

9 Two special long **challot** are used for the festival meal in the home. Why do you think this is done?

10 Design a **poster for Shavuot** including as many ideas from the festival as you can.

SHAVUOT ASSESSMENT

1 When does **Shavuot** take place?

2 What is the **'Counting of the Omer'**?

3 Name **TWO foods** traditional for this festival.

4 Give **TWO reasons** for the eating of **dairy foods** at this festival.

5 Shavuot is sometimes called *Atseret*, which means **'stop'**. It is also known as the **end of Passover**. Why do you think this is so?

6 Why does the **Torah** have such a special importance in Jewish life and belief?

7 What is the special reason for **studying and praying** all night on Shavuot?

8 What is the connection between the **story of Ruth** and **Shavuot**?

9 For what reason do children sometimes begin their **Hebrew classes** at Shavuot?

10 What is the **three-cornered kreplach** said to represent?

11 Shavuot is the **least known** of the major Jewish festivals. Why do you think this is so?

12 Describe the special **Sefardi tradition** of the marriage contract at Shavuot. What does this suggest about the attitude of Jews to their religion?

 # Rosh Hashanah

INTRODUCTION

Rosh Hashanah (head of the year) is celebrated on 1 and 2 Tishri.

The month of Elul, which precedes Rosh Hashanah, is called *Teshuvah* – the month of repentance. During this time people begin to think about repenting for their misdeeds over the past year. From the first day of Elul until the 28th (excluding the Sabbaths) the *shofar*, a ram's horn, is blown each morning in the synagogue. The blasts on the shofar are the same for Elul as they are for Rosh Hashanah:

Tekiah – one long call
Shevarim – three short calls (a broken heart)
Teruah – nine quick calls (an alarm)

The shofar recalls the Revelation on Mount Sinai:

And it came to pass on the third day, when it was morning, that there were thunders and lightnings and a thick cloud upon the mount, and the voice of a horn exceeding loud.

Exodus 19:16

The shofar also heralded the *Jubilee* (Leviticus 25) a fifty-year cycle when, at the end of each cycle, slaves were freed and land returned to its original owners.

Many people visit the graves of their relatives during Elul. Teshuvah is a time to apologize for mistakes made and hurt caused during the year.

The days from Rosh Hashanah to Yom Kippur are sometimes known as the *High Holy Days*. In Hebrew they are known as *Yamim Noraim* – the days of awe – or the ten days of penitence – *Aseret Yemai Teshuvah*.

Rosh Hashanah has three meanings;

1 Tradition says that it is the anniversary of the Creation.
2 The Torah calls it *Yom Teruah* – the day of shofar sounding.
3 The Rabbis called it *Yom Hadin* – the day of judgement.

Stories and Legends

Tradition says that on the Rosh Hashanah, God forgave Adam his sins.

Maimonides gave the following reasons for the use of the shofar: it is curved to show that the Jews submit to God's will and his moulding; it is held to the right pointing upwards so that the message goes from the heart to God; it is blown at the narrow end to show that thoughts (sound) emerge from a broad mind and heart.

The Torah readings for the two days are:
Genesis 21 and 22 – the birth and sacrifice of Isaac.
Numbers 29:1–6 – the instruction to celebrate the day.
I Samuel 1:1–2:10 – the story of Hannah and the gift of the child Samuel.
Jeremiah 31:2–20 – Rachel weeping for the children of Israel.

The three passages are about the love of three mothers, Sarah, Hannah and Rachel, and the sacrifices which are made. The stories are about faith and the acceptance of God's power.

Sources

The command to keep the festival is in Numbers 29. All the teachings associated with the festival are in the Torah, the Writings, the Prophets and Talmud.

Location

The home and the synagogue. Somewhere outside near running water for Tashlich.

Ritual

During Elul people may greet one another with:

May you be inscribed (in the Book of Life) *for a good year.*

After morning prayers on Rosh Hashanah the ceremony of *Hatarat Nedarim* takes place in the synagogue. The men there form a beth din and annul each other's vows. This is done because it is likely that during the past year each person will have broken at least one vow.

Cooking is permitted on Rosh Hashanah but lighting a flame is not, so cookers, if they do not have a pilot light, are left turned on.

At the family meal the challah is dipped in honey instead of being sprinkled with salt.

Slices of apple are dipped in honey and God is asked to grant 'a good and sweet year'.

In the synagogue, before the Torah is returned to the Ark, the shofar is sounded thirty times. Then during the *Mussaf* section of the service it is sounded again, ten times for each section:

Malchuyot – God's rule over the world.
Zichronot – good deeds of ancestors.
Shofarot – revelation and redemption.

Finally at the end of the service another forty calls are made.

TASHLICH
This ritual takes place in the afternoon. People stand beside water and recite a prayer, symbolically throwing their sins into the water:

And Thou wilt cast all their sins into the depths of the sea.

Micah 7:19

The following day, 3 Tishri, *Tzom Gedaliah*, a fast from dawn to dusk to remember the murder of the governor of Judaea in the sixth century B.C.E. It marked the end of the Jewish community in Jerusalem after the destruction of the first Temple.

Artefacts
New clothes – worn on Rosh Hashanah to celebrate the happiness of a new year. Shofar. Greetings cards–thesearecombinedforthetendaysofrepentanceand wish people 'a good year and well over the fast'. (See *Living Festivals – Rosh Hashanah and Yom Kippur*.)

Food
The importance of food at Rosh Hashanah is that it should be sweet so that the sweetness may be carried forward into the next year.

Special round challot are made with honey (sometimes raisins are added).

Honey cakes are made as is nollent (honey pastry made with dried fruit and cherries).

The head of a fish is cooked for the first course, though it may not be eaten. This is so that: 'You may be a head instead of a tail'.

Tzimmes (sweet carrots) are eaten. In Yiddish carrots are *merin* but the word also means increase: 'May you increase'.

Significant Persons
All people, Sarah, Abraham, Isaac, Hannah, Samuel, Rachel.

Yom Kippur

INTRODUCTION

Yom Kippur falls at the end of the ten days of repentance on 10 Tishri. It is the day on which the verdict on a person's behaviour in the past year is sealed in the Book of Life. From now until ten days later on *Hoshanah Rabbah*, when final sealing takes place, the greeting changes to:

> *May a good sealing complete your inscription.*

Yom Kippur is also called *Shabbat Shabbaton* – the ultimate of Sabbaths.

After seeking forgiveness from their family, friends and neighbours, people are free to atone with God and to ask his forgiveness.

Stories and Legends

The commandment to fast on this day is derived from a passage in Leviticus 16:29:

> *... in the seventh month on the tenth day of the month, ye shall afflict your souls.*

Here is also found the story of the scapegoat.

The connection between affliction and fasting is taken from Isaiah 58:3:

> *Wherefore have we fasted, and Thou seest not? Wherefore have we afflicted our souls, and Thou takest no knowledge.*

In the days of the Temple a bull and goat were sacrificed for Yom Kippur and the scapegoat, on which the sins of the people were laid, was driven out of the city. This was the one day of the year on which the High Priest entered the Holy of Holies, where he begged forgiveness for the people's sins.

Sources

Readings are taken from the Torah and Prophets:

> *Leviticus 16* – the scapegoat.
> *Leviticus 18* – the importance of *living* the Torah.
> *Numbers 29* – the Temple services for Yom Kippur.
> *Isaiah 57–58* – fasting is meaningless without inward thought.
> *Jonah* – human suffering and God's willingness to forgive everyone.

Location

The home and especially the synagogue.

Ritual

On the day before Yom Kippur some men go to the mikvah (the ritual bath) to cleanse themselves fully for the day.

KAPPARAH

On Erev Yom Kippur (the day before the fast) people used to take a live hen or fish into the home. The father waved it three times over the head of each of the family saying:

> *'This is in exchange for you. This is in place of you. This is your atonement. This chicken will go to its death, but you will go on to a good and long life and to peace.'*

This was done to replace the scapegoat which had originally been sacrificed for the sins of the community. Modern Jews usually replace the animals with a handful of notes which are then given to charity.

Before the beginning of Yom Kippur at sunset, there is a mitzvah meal (one which must be eaten). After this the festival candles are lit and the fast has begun. Yahrzeit candles are often lit for dead relatives at this time. Children are blessed that they may be sealed in the Book of Life and Happiness. Also parents and children may ask forgiveness of each other for what they have done during the year.

As well as all the Sabbath restrictions there are five additional ones attached to Yom Kippur, all of which apply for twenty-five hours:

1 no food or drink (this is lifted either for young children or if it will cause danger to health). Four reasons for this fasting are given:
   (a) it shows a sincere desire for forgiveness.
   (b) it shows self-discipline which can be applied to the character.
   (c) it allows concentration on the spirit.
   (d) it makes the person more compassionate.
2 no washing (except of hands after using the lavatory).
3 no anointing, e.g. applying make-up.

4 no leather shoes – to wear the skin of a dead animal would not be right when asking God's mercy for all creatures.

5 no sexual intercourse.

In the synagogue there are five services instead of the usual three.

The haunting song *Kol Nidrei* – 'All our vows' – is sung. There is a general confession – *Al Chet* – 'For the sin of ...'. This lists forty-four sins and the people beat their breasts with each one. People recite this together using 'we' so that no one need feel isolated.

The final service of the day is *Ne'ilah* – sealing or closing. At the end of this service the opening verse of the Shema is said by the congregation:

Hear O Israel: the Lord our God, the Lord is One.

Three times this blessing is repeated:

Blessed be his name, whose glorious Kingdom is for ever and ever.

The reader and the congregation repeat seven times:

The Lord, he is God

Finally there is one long call on the shofar.

Many people have stayed all day at the synagogue. They now return home to break their fast and start their preparations for Succot, which is four days away.

Artefacts

The synagogue is dressed in white (the colour of purity and atonement); the Ark curtains are white and there is a white covering over the chazzan's reading desk.

Men wear white kapels. Some wear a full white robe like a shroud and known as a kittel. Also on this one occasion of the year, men wear their tallits for the evening service.

Food

The last meal on Erev Yom Kippur is a mitzvah. The fasting lasts for twenty-five hours.

Significant Persons

The Jewish people.

THEMES FOR THE CLASSROOM

Rosh Hashanah

1 The principal theme for the festivals of Rosh Hashanah and Yom Kippur are those of repentance and forgiveness. First people ask each other for forgiveness and then repenting, they ask God to forgive them and to allow them to make a fresh start with the New Year.

2 The greatness of God's bounty and the need to offer service to him is made clear in the Torah readings for Rosh Hashanah. The various instances of goodness and service mentioned in the readings can be taken up and discussed.

3 Rosh Hashanah is said to be the anniversary of Creation. Like the gift of the Torah, Creation is another example of God's bounty. Teachers might wish to look at God's role in Creation as it is recounted in the Torah.

Yom Kippur

1 Yom Kippur is the most holy day of the year; a final attempt at reconciliation with God. The importance of asking forgiveness is particularly stressed at Yom Kippur when parents and children ask forgiveness of God and each other. The idea of repentance and forgiveness and the ways in which these can be demonstrated could be discussed here with pupils of any age. Older pupils might consider whether these practices are primarily for the benefit of God or for the good which they do to the participants.

2 Fasting and other restrictions are very important features of the festival and the way in which they are undertaken should be considered. Teachers might wish to look at fasting in other religious traditions and consider the various reasons behind the practice. (See *Living Festivals – Shrove Tuesday, Ash Wednesday and Mardi Gras*.)

3 'White' as a symbol of purity. Why is it chosen and what is the importance of colour in religious worship?

THE WORKSHEETS

The first worksheet is a piece of work producing a display on the Creation.

This is followed by a piece of imaginative writing on 'Mothers in the Bible'.

There is a Wordsquare and Wordsearch on Rosh Hashanah and Yom Kippur and then a test and full assessment.

N.B. In question 10 of the test the teacher may feel the need to ensure some privacy for the pupils and not, for example, ask them to read out what they have written.

THE STORY OF CREATION

You will find the Biblical story of Creation at the beginning of the Book of Genesis, the first book of the Bible.

On this page you will find 5 pictures which show some of the things which were created.

Read the story of Creation from the Bible (Genesis 1:1 – 2:3). Now, put the Bible away and rewrite the story using your own words to describe what happened.

When you have finished your account of the Creation copy it out on to a large sheet of paper. Put a large heading – **The Creation**. Colour in the pictures on this page, cut them out and then stick them in the right places on your display.

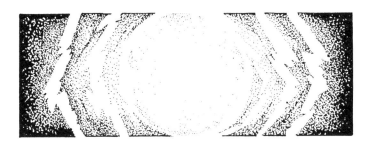

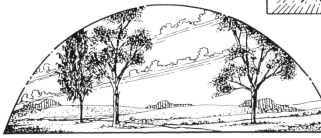

MOTHERS IN THE BIBLE

Three of the readings for Rosh Hashanah are about mothers:

Sarah – Genesis 21 and 22

Hannah – 1 Samuel 1:1 – 2:10

Rachel – Jeremiah 31:2–20

Choose **ONE** of these women. Read the passage in the Bible.
Write and illustrate the story as though you were the woman concerned. Try to imagine how you would have felt and what your reactions would be to the situation in which she found herself.

ROSH HASHANAH AND YOM KIPPUR WORDSQUARE

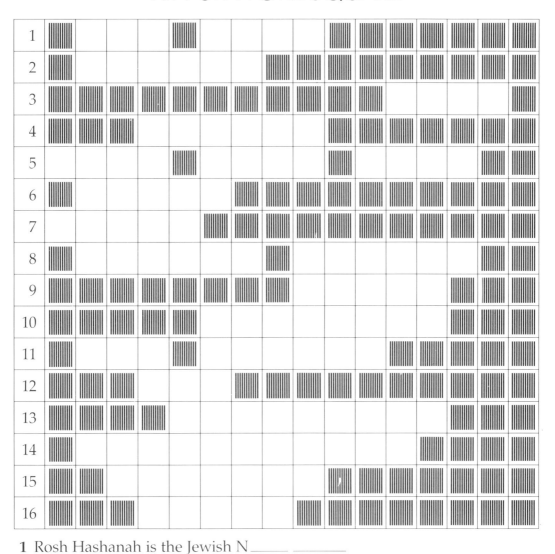

1 Rosh Hashanah is the Jewish N_____ _____

2 It takes place on the 1 and 2 T_____

3 The month of repentance before Rosh Hashanah is called E_____

4 Each morning the S_____ is blown in the synagogue

5 The days from Rosh Hashanah to Yom Kippur are sometimes called the H_____ _____ _____

6 Rosh Hashanah is said to be the day on which the W_____ was created

7 Three women are remembered in the synagogue readings; these are; S_____

8 H_____ and R_____

9 At the family meal the challah is dipped in H_____

10 In the afternoon people perform T_____ to get rid of their sins

11 The ten days of repentance end with Y_____ _____

12 People ask G_____ to forgive them

13 In the past the S_____ was driven out of the Temple at this time

14 People fast for T_____ hours

15 They do not wash or wear L_____

16 On this day the synagogue is decorated in W_____

61

ROSH HASHANAH AND YOM KIPPUR WORDSEARCH

J	S	E	M	M	I	Z	T	E	S	H	U	V	A	H	R	E
O	R	R	K	I	T	T	E	L	A	M	I	K	V	A	H	J
N	Y	O	M	K	I	P	P	U	R	E	W	F	F	I	S	H
A	T	S	E	S	S	U	T	L	E	T	I	H	W	K	O	C
H	I	H	J	S	H	O	F	A	R	Y	B	N	I	E	R	I
A	R	H	O	U	R	L	O	P	H	A	U	R	E	T	N	L
I	U	A	S	H	E	V	A	R	I	M	K	L	U	K	E	H
L	P	S	T	U	I	U	H	E	B	I	O	G	H	A	T	S
A	R	H	M	Y	L	O	H	V	E	M	I	N	A	P	A	A
D	Z	A	X	W	N	I	R	E	M	N	U	I	N	P	O	T
E	S	N	C	A	T	N	E	L	L	O	N	T	N	A	G	S
G	E	A	S	H	R	Y	D	A	S	R	M	S	A	R	E	E
M	A	H	U	I	E	R	Y	T	S	A	R	A	H	A	P	L
O	L	U	Q	N	L	L	S	I	R	I	F	F	E	H	A	P
Z	E	U	O	G	H	A	N	O	J	M	R	W	T	V	C	P
T	D	H	T	N	E	M	E	N	O	T	A	R	E	T	S	A

ROSH HASHANAH	SEALED	AWE
SHEVARIM	SCAPEGOAT	APPLES
TZOM GEDALIAH	HANNAH	TASHLICH
REVELATION	HONEY	KITTEL
TERUAH	FISH	SHOFAR
ELUL	WHITE	SAMUEL
MERIN	JONAH	SARAH
FASTING	TESHUVAH	NOLLENT
HOLY	RACHEL	TZIMMES
YOM KIPPUR	NORAIM	KAPPARAH
YAMIM	TEKIAH	PURITY

ROSH HASHANAH AND YOM KIPPUR TEST

1 What do people do during the month of **Elul**?

2 What common name is often given to **Rosh Hashanah**?

3 What is **Yom Kippur** usually called in English?

4 What **colour** is usually associated with Yom Kippur and what does it stand for?

5 What do Jews do **without** on Yom Kippur?

6 What **musical instrument** is played at these festivals?

7 Name TWO of the three **mothers** whose story is read at this time.

8 What is the traditional **greeting** for Rosh Hashanah?

9 Sort out these words which are associated with the festivals:

yoneh	horat	gapescaot
lesdanc	telkit	lok ridein
hatreel	ginstaf	pakharap
chilshat		

10 Do you think that this period of saying you are sorry to people is a good idea? What particular things do you think that someone of your age might want to apologize for?

ROSH HASHANAH AND YOM KIPPUR ASSESSMENT

1 Why do you think that the days from Rosh Hashanah to Yom Kippur are sometimes called the **High Holy Days**?

2 What is **Tashlich**?

3 **Kapparah** appears to be a very ancient tradition. What do you think is its significance today?

4 Describe a **shofar**. What is its use and importance?

5 The ten days of **Awe** or **Repentance** are still very important to Jews. Can you suggest reasons for this?

6 Whose sins were **forgiven** by God on Rosh Hashanah according to tradition?

7 Why do people wear **white** on Yom Kippur?

8 Why is **sweet food** eaten at Rosh Hashanah?

9 Yom Kippur is sometimes called **Shabbat Shabbaton** – the ultimate Sabbath. Why is this name so suitable for the day?

10 What is the importance of **fasting** on Yom Kippur?

11 What **customs** were associated with Yom Kippur at the time of the Temple?

12 Today many people might feel that some of these ceremonies and events are **old-fashioned and superstitious**. Discuss this idea and give reasons for your opinion.

Succot

INTRODUCTION

Succot (Festival of Tabernacles) begins four days after Yom Kippur, on 15 Tishri, and continues until 22 Tishri. It is the third harvest festival of the year when the Jews travelled to the Temple in Jerusalem. The festival also represents the journey through the desert after the Exodus (*Living Festivals – Succot*, pp. 16–21).

Succah (pl. succot) means hut, booth or tabernacle. 'Succot' refers to the temporary shelters in which the Jews lived in the desert. Also, farmers gathering in the final harvest lived in booths at the edge of the fields so that they did not have to journey home each night.

There is a connection between the richness of the harvest and the temporariness of living in the succah. When people feel safe they leave the security of their homes and look up through the roof of the succah in the knowledge of the permanent security of God's care.

The festival is also known as *Zman Simhatenu* – the Season for Our Rejoicing. Three times in the Torah the Jews are told to rejoice on Succot.

The first two and last two days are festival days on which no work other than food preparation is done.

The third to sixth days of the festival are *Chol Hamoed* – weekdays of the festival. During this time all work, except that which is necessary is avoided. For the remaining days of the festival, see *Shemini Atseret* and *Simchat Torah*, pages 67 and 68.

The 21st day of Tishri is *Hoshanah Rabbah* – the day of Hosanna. Many Jews stay up until after midnight on this day reading the Torah.

The days of Succot

Tishri 15	16	17	18	19	20	21	22	23
Succot	Simchat Bet Hashoeva	Chol Hamoed				Hoshanah Rabbah	Shemini Atseret	Simchat Torah

Stories and Legends

The principal story associated with Succot is of the Israelites wandering in the wilderness and building temporary huts for themselves.

Seventy sacrifices were ordered for the Temple during Succot. These were said to be atonement offerings made by the Jews on behalf of the seventy nations of the earth. The tradition of hospitality to non-Jews during the festival is an anticipation of the time in which Zechariah said that non-Jews would travel to Jerusalem for Succot.

Hoshanah Rabbah is the day on which tradition says that the heavenly court finally seals the book of judgement that was finished on Yom Kippur. (See *Living Festivals – Succot and Simchat Torah*, p. 12.)

Sources
Leviticus 23:33–43
Zechariah 14:16–17
The date of the events in the desert is about 1250 B.C.E.

Location
Originally the desert, now the succah at home or at the synagogue.

Ritual
The mitzvah is to live in the succah for seven days but an extra day is added in the Diaspora. Most people eat in the succah but they do not usually sleep in it. At Succot people try to invite guests to eat with them especially people who do not have a succah of their own. People do not eat in the succah if it is raining or if they themselves are ill. You cannot rejoice in the succah when you are suffering.

Each morning of the festival, except on the Sabbath, people take up their lulav and etrog (see *Living Festivals – Succot and Simchat Torah*, pp. 10–13). They hold the lulav in their right hand and the etrog in their left (pittam down) (see illustration on p. 71) then join their hands together and say the blessing. After this the etrog is turned upside down. The lulav and etrog are then waved in six directions: front (east), right, back, left, up and down. This shows God's power all over the universe, heaven and earth.

The lulav and etrog are also taken to the synagogue. Here, after the Musaf, the chazzan carries the Torah scroll around the outer aisles and is joined by a procession of men holding their lulavs. This is called *Hoshanot* as the Hoshanah prayer (Help Us) is sung during the procession.

The second day of the festival is similar. In Israel, before the destruction of the Temple, the festival of

Simchat Bet Hashoeva was held. Water was drawn from the Pool of Siloam and splashed all over the altar of the Temple. All the menorah in the city were lit and there were carnival-like processions with Rabbis performing acrobatics and juggling with torches. On Hoshanah Rabbah, 20 Tishri, the ark and the bimah are again covered in white and the Rabbi and chazzan wear kittels. After Musaf the Hoshanot procession begins. Seven scrolls are carried around the synagogue in seven processions each followed by men carrying a lulav and etrog. They sing chants with the theme Hosannah – Help Us.

On Hoshanah Rabbah the prayer is for water. The men beat willow branches on the ground three times until some of the leaves fall off. It is done to remind God of what happens when there is not enough water. Also it is said to be the shedding of sins. Hoshanah Rabbah is the last morning for waving the lulav and etrog. After this they are not thrown away but often left outside to return naturally to the earth.

Artefacts

Ye shall dwell in booths seven days; all that are home-born in Israel shall dwell in booths.

Leviticus 23:42

The principal artefact of the festival is the succah. It is built outside the home or the synagogue. It must not be huge but large enough to accommodate the family who will use it. Building cannot start until after Yom Kippur and must be complete by the beginning of the festival.

The walls of the succah can be built of almost anything, but the roof, the *s'chah*, must be natural and be cut specially for the purpose; thus the branches of an overhanging tree cannot be used. Also the roof must cast more shade than the sun but must also allow the light of the stars to shine through. The roof must be the last thing to be put in place. The succah is not blessed because the mitzvah is to live in it not to build it.

The interior is decorated with cards, fruit, paper decorations, etc., and *ushpizzin*, pictures or signs bearing the names of the Jewish forefathers who are invited, one each day, into the succah:

Abraham, Isaac, Jacob, Joseph, Moses, Aaron and David.

LULAV AND ETROG
(*Living Festivals – Succot*, pp. 10–13 and 22–23.)

And ye shall take you on the first day the fruit of goodly trees, branches of palm-trees, and boughs of thick trees, and willows of the brook, and ye shall rejoice before the LORD *seven days.*

Leviticus 23:40

The lulav and etrog therefore together have four components:

Hadas – etrog
Lulav – palm
Myrtle
Aravah – willow

The etrog is a citrus fruit which looks like a lemon but tastes and smells quite different, and it has a pittam or pistil. Without this it is not kosher.

The palm, willow and myrtle are placed in a woven palm holder to form the lulav. The etrog is held in the same hand as the lulav. There are various reasons given for the choice of these four. Presumably they were intended to symbolize the final bringing in of the harvest but they are also said to be representative of other things:

Etrog	Palm	Myrtle	Willow
Psalm 104:1	Psalm 92:12	Zechariah 1:8	Psalm 68:4
Each of these species is an allusion to God as in these verses			
The four species represent the four-letter name of God			
heart – understanding	spine – uprightness	eyes – enlightenment	mouth – prayer
yellow – fire	grows into the sky – air	grows near the ground – earth	grows beside rivers – water
They are said to represent goodness and learning; either by symbolizing use and beauty or by their own smell and taste. In this way they refer to the way in which four types of people respond to the Torah and their acts of goodness and religious duty			
beautiful and useful	useful but not beautiful	beautiful but not useful	neither useful nor beautiful
taste and smell	taste and no smell	smell but no taste	neither taste nor smell

CLOTHES
By tradition a husband should purchase new clothing for his wife for Succot.

Food
There are no food requirements for Succot except that meals are eaten in the succah.

Significant Persons
The Jews gathering in the harvest and travelling through the desert.

Shemini Atseret

INTRODUCTION

Shemini Atseret is on 22 Tishri. The word 'atseret' means 'conclusion'. It is the concluding day of Succot and also a festival in its own right. It is a day of rest when no work is done. Jews continue to live in the succah until lunchtime but do not say the succah blessing.

Stories and Legends

The festival, along with the rest of Succot, relates to the Israelites in the wilderness.

Sources

The readings for the day are:

Deuteronomy 14:22 – 16:17
Numbers 29:35 – 30:1
I Kings 8:54 – 66

The Torah passage for the day is about tithing and is a reminder to the congregation that they should not come to festivals empty-handed:

*… and they shall not appear before the L*ORD* empty; every man shall give as he is able, according to the blessing of the* L*ORD* thy God which He hath given thee.*

Deuteronomy 16:16–17

Date is about 1250 B.C.E.

Location

The home and the synagogue.

Ritual

The important feature of the festival is the prayer for rain *Tefilat Geshem*. The Rabbis decided that people did not want rain while they were living in the succah so the prayer is delayed until the last day:

May He send rain from the heavenly source to soften the earth with its crystal drops …

Siddur

From this time until the first day of Passover the following prayer is said:

Thou causest the wind to blow and the rain to fall.

The prayer is added to the blessing

Thou, O Lord, art mighty for ever, thou revivest the dead, thou art mighty to save.

Siddur

So a connection is made between rain and resurrection, both restoring life.

Artefacts

None.

Food

No particular requirements but meals are still eaten in the succah.

Significant Persons

The Israelites in the wilderness.

Simchat Torah

INTRODUCTION

Simchat Torah – the rejoicing in the Torah – is on 23 Tishri. It takes place on the ninth day of Succot in the Diaspora but is reckoned as a separate festival. It celebrates the completion of the yearly reading of the Torah and the beginning of the new cycle of readings.

Stories and Legends

Originally the completion of the Torah readings occurred on the second day of Shemini Atseret and this was called 'the day of the book', but the eleventh century *Prayerbook of Rashi* refers to it as Simchat Torah.

Sources

Deuteronomy 33:1 – 34:12
Genesis 1:1 – 2:3
Numbers 29:35 – 30:1
Joshua 1: 1–18
The origins of the festival are medieval.

Location

The synagogue.

Ritual

(*Living Festivals – Succot and Simchat Torah*, pp. 14–15.)
At the evening service all the Torah scrolls are taken from the ark and the chazzan says:

Please, Lord, save us. Please, Lord, make us succeed.

The scrolls are then carried around the synagogue seven times (seven *hakafot* – circuits) while the congregation sing songs and dance with the Torah. Children carry flags with apples on top and are sometimes given sweets as they go around in procession. All but one of the scrolls are replaced in the ark then the last passage of Deuteronomy is read from the remaining one. This is the only time that the Torah is read in the synagogue in the evening.

At the morning services the seven circuits are repeated. As many men as possible are given an *aliyah* (called up to the Torah) to say the blessing

Blessed art thou, O Lord our God, King of the universe, who has chosen us from all nations and given us thy Law. Blessed art thou, O Lord, who givest the Law.

Siddur

In some communities one of the seven circuits is dedicated to prayer for Jews in the Soviet Union.

Near the end of the readings all the children, *Kol Ha'ne'arim*, are brought together and large prayer shawls are held over them. The children then recite the aliyah blessing with an adult. This is followed by Jacob's blessing:

. . . the angel who hath redeemed me from all evil, bless the children; and let my name be named in them, and the name of my fathers Abraham and Isaac; and let them grow into a multitude in the midst of the earth.

Genesis 48:16

After this the congregation sing:

And you shall see children born to your children. Let there be peace in Israel.

This is followed by the final three aliyot. These are recited by the two *chattanim* – the two bridegrooms. These are two people who are well known for their work in the community and who were announced at Yom Kippur. Again the tallit may be held over them as they read, symbolizing the chuppah. The first portion goes to the *chattan Torah* – groom of the Torah – who reads the end of Deuteronomy; the second passage is for the *chattan Bereshit* – groom of Genesis – and is the story of Creation; the final part is read by another reader and describes Joshua taking over from Moses.

The readings thus show how the Torah returns and goes on for ever and how the human chain is continued as well.

Sometimes the chazzan may be replaced for Simchat Torah by a lay chazzan who will sing the prayers to modern tunes. There is a carnival atmosphere of celebration in the synagogue at this time.

Artefacts

Seven Torah scrolls, tallit.

Food

Sweets for children.

Significant Persons

Chazzan, chattanim. The community.

THEMES FOR THE CLASSROOM

These three festivals present a wealth of ideas for classroom topics.

Succot

1 Thanksgiving for harvest and the offering of the fruits of the harvest to God.

2 Work on the travels of the Israelites through the wilderness.

3 Giving up security in life to trust in God's mercy by living in the succah.

4 Rejoicing in God's bounty.

5 The Jewish hope of unity with all people – the hospitality offered in the succah (Zechariah's prophecy of non-Jews going to the Temple for Succot).

6 The many-layered symbolism of the lulav and etrog.

Hoshanah Rabbah

1 Now, thanking God for the gift of water.

2 Reminding themselves of how valuable and necessary water is for life.

Shemini Atseret

1 A reminder that it is the duty of people who have food and wealth to:
   (a)   look after those less well off than themselves.
   (b)   offer part of their riches back to God.

2 The value of rain and the reliance of life on continuing rain. Here there is an opportunity to look at the problems which arise in those countries with insufficient rain such as parts of North Africa.

Simchat Torah

1 Giving thanks to God for the revelation of the Torah. As well as being a thanksgiving, this is also a reminder of the value of the Torah, which has guided the Jews for over 3000 years. This is so important that the event becomes almost a carnival as people show their joy in the Torah by dancing with the scrolls.

   How does the way in which Jews think of the Torah compare with the approach of other religions to their sacred books?

2 Stress is laid on the eternal nature of the Torah as its reading is completed and started again. Also made clear is the fact that people must die but the human chain will continue; so, as Moses died, his place was taken by Joshua.

3 The importance of educating children in the Torah and the ways of their religion. Also the importance which children see for themselves in carrying on the faith and the Jewish people.

4 The suffering of the Jewish people through pogroms and anti-Semite persecution, in particular Russian Jewry.

THE WORKSHEETS

The first two worksheets describe how to make a model succah and a lulav.

   These are followed by a Wordsearch on the festival of Succot and then by a test and full assessment.

MAKING A SUCCAH

This picture shows a succah. Carefully colour it in.
Now you are going to make a model succah for yourself.

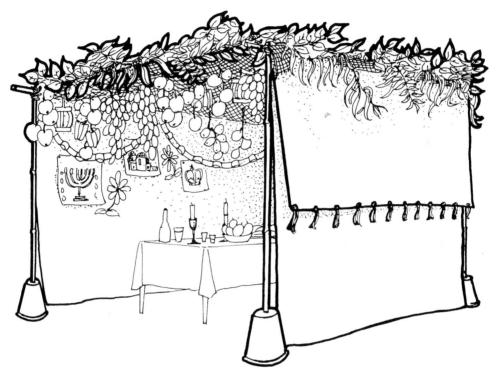

MATERIALS

piece of wood approx 15 cm × 10 cm × 1 cm
lollipop sticks or art straws
raffia or strips of paper
glue or small nails
twigs

1 Fix the lollipop sticks or art straws with glue or nails around three sides of the piece of wood.

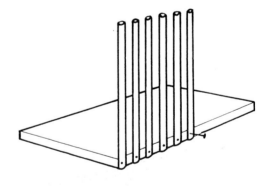

2 Weave the raffia or paper through the sticks.

3 Lay the twigs across the top of the sticks as a roof (remember the stars have to be seen through the roof so it does not need to be too thick).

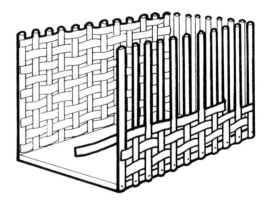

4 Make small ushpizzin (pictures of the prophets) and miniature fruit to hang inside.

5 You can also make miniature chairs and tables out of folded card to put inside.

6 The base can be painted to look like earth or grass.

MAKING A LULAV

The waving of the lulav is a very important part of Succot. These instructions show you how to make a lulav using some natural materials and some artificial ones.

MATERIALS

*large sheet of green card at least 60 cm long and
    80 cm wide*
willow twigs 40–50 cm long
*myrtle twigs or twigs from a similar tree or bush
    e.g. privet*
a sheet of thin card
a lemon
raffia

1 Cut the card into ten strips approx. 60 cm × 8 cm.

2 Draw the outline of the palm leaf on each and cut them out.

3 Lay the 'leaves' on top of each other and bind the end with raffia to make a firm stalk (see Fig. 1).

4 Cut out a piece of card approx 30 cm × 8 cm.

5 Score lines along the length of the card, stopping 1 cm from the end (see Fig. 2).

6 Cut the rest of the card into strips 1 cm wide and begin to weave them as shown in the diagram.

7 Glue the ends of each strip down very securely.

8 Fold the woven card in half along its length.

9 Hold the 'palm', the myrtle and willow together and wrap the holder around them securing it with raffia (see Fig. 3).

10 The lulav is held in the right hand and the etrog in the left. If you wave the lulav it should make a sound like dry palm fronds beating together.

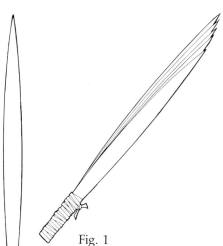

Fig. 1

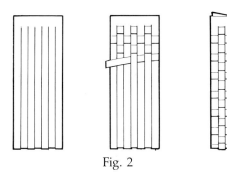

Fig. 2

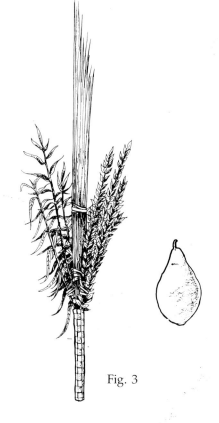

Fig. 3

SUCCOT, SHEMINI ATSERET AND SIMCHAT TORAH WORDSEARCH

C	A	M	E	H	S	E	G	H	A	L	I	F	E	T	Y	P
A	S	Y	H	A	B	B	A	R	H	A	N	A	H	S	O	H
A	E	R	S	U	C	C	O	T	O	R	A	H	A	C	H	A
S	S	T	U	H	A	H	O	A	I	R	S	W	V	H	A	K
I	O	L	C	B	N	O	P	B	F	S	D	F	A	A	R	A
H	M	E	C	V	C	L	O	E	H	T	H	I	R	H	O	F
A	B	D	A	V	H	H	M	R	P	H	O	R	A	S	T	O
Y	M	L	H	A	A	A	A	N	E	O	S	E	I	P	T	T
I	U	A	R	C	I	M	H	A	S	O	H	P	R	I	A	N
L	S	E	E	O	R	O	A	C	O	B	A	F	G	T	H	A
A	S	E	T	B	A	E	R	L	J	L	N	Y	O	O	C	T
S	A	D	A	H	H	D	B	E	M	Y	O	R	R	M	M	T
I	F	O	W	E	C	T	A	S	E	R	T	O	T	U	I	A
N	M	T	E	R	E	S	T	A	I	N	I	M	E	H	S	H
A	S	C	N	I	Z	Z	I	P	H	S	U	R	E	M	N	C
I	P	E	R	G	N	I	H	T	I	T	W	O	L	L	I	W

SUCCOT	TITHING	HADAS
HOSHANAH RABBAH	LULAV	SINAI
PITOM	USHPIZZIN	JOSEPH
SIMCHAT TORAH	WILLOW	AIR
HAKAFOT	JACOB	HOSHANOT
ZECHARIAH	WATER	SUCCAH
CHATTAN	CHOL HAMOED	HUTS
ARAVAH	SHEMINI ATSERET	TORAH
ISAAC	ALIYAH	SCHAH
FIRE	PALM	MYRTLE
TABERNACLES	TISHRI	ABRAHAM
TEFILAH GESHEM	BOOTHS	MOSES
MUSSAF		

SUCCOT AND SIMCHAT TORAH TEST

1 What **other name** does this festival have?

2 When does it **take place**?

3 What is a **succah**?

4 What **TWO** things does this festival **celebrate**?

5 Why is **hospitality** given especially to non-Jews at this festival?

6 Describe a **lulav** and **etrog**. How are they used?

7 Complete this table.

Etrog	Palm	Myrtle	Willow
The four species represent the four-letter name of _____			
_____ – understanding	spine – uprightness	eyes – enlightenment	mouth – _____
yellow = fire	grows into the sky = _____	grows near the ground = _____	grows beside rivers = water
beautiful and useful	useful but not _____	_____ but not useful	neither useful nor beautiful
taste ___ ___	taste and no smell	smell but no taste	neither taste ___ ___

8 What are **ushpizzin**?

9 Why is the roof of a succah **not solid** even in a country where there is a lot of rain?

10 Describe a synagogue service on **Simchat Torah**.

SUCCOT, SHEMINI ATSERET AND SIMCHAT TORAH ASSESSMENT

1 What **TWO** events does **Succot celebrate?**

2 What event is said to take place on the seventh day of Succot – Hoshanah Rabbah?

3 Why must the **roof** of a succah not be made of a material such as polythene or iron?

4 People are told to live in the succah. Why is this requirement lifted if they are **ill** or it is **raining**?

5 Describe the **construction** and **use** of the lulav and etrog.

6 Give **ONE** explanation of the significance of the **lulav** and **etrog**.

7 What special prayer is said on **Shemini Atseret**?

8 What purpose do you think is served by building a succah and living in it?

9 What does **Simchat Torah** celebrate?

10 What is important about the **Torah readings** on Simchat Torah?

11 What special part do **children** play in the service for Simchat Torah?

12 Try to explain why people dance with the scrolls at this festival.

Chanukah

INTRODUCTION

Chanukah begins on 25 Kislev. It celebrates the repossession of the Temple after its desecration by the Greeks, led by Antiochus Epiphanes. The Maccabees or Hasmoneans cleaned and purified the Temple, rebuilt and rededicated the altar and relit the six-foot-high, golden, seven-branched Great Menorah. It was on 25 Kislev 165 B.C.E. that Judah the Maccabee offered *Korban Tamid*, the daily sacrifice. (The story is told in *Living Festivals – Chanukah*.) The reason for the festival being celebrated over eight days is not clear and there are several explanations:

1 The original dedication of the first Temple took seven days and the people left on the eighth.

2 The story of the oil which is found in the Talmud.

3 The fact that the Jews had been deprived of celebrating Succot and Shemini Atseret (q.v.) and had vowed, three months earlier in the mountains, that they would do so as soon as they reclaimed the Temple:

And they kept eight days with gladness, as in the feast of the tabernacles, remembering that not long afore they had held the feast of the tabernacles, when as they wandered in the mountains and dens like beasts ... They ordained also by a common statute and decree, that every year those days should be kept of the whole nation of the Jews.

II Maccabees 6, 8

Chanukah is a mid-winter festival of light and a time to give presents.

Although the festival marks a victory of the Jews over their oppressors, the readings make clear that it is God who has caused the victory:

Not by might, nor by power, but by My Spirit, saith the LORD *of hosts.*

Stories and Legends

On the 25th day of Kislev, the days of the Chanukah festival begin. There are eight days, during which eulogies for the dead and fasting are prohibited. When the Greeks entered the Temple, they defiled all the oil stored in it. After the *Hasmoneans had established their rule and prevailed, they searched and found one single cruse of oil, still sealed with the seal of the High Priest. But there was only enough oil to last for one day. A miracle occurred, and the supply lasted for eight days. In the following year, they appointed these days as festival days, with the recitation of Hallel and with thanksgiving.*

Talmud – Shabbat 21B

This particular story is not found in the Book of Maccabees but only in the Talmud. This is the reason that Chanukah became known as *Chag Ha'Urim* – the holiday of the miracle of lights.

Sources

The story of the Maccabees and their fight to reclaim the Temple is found in the apocryphal Book of Maccabees. These events took place in about 165 B.C.E. (*Living Festivals – Chanukah*, p. 13 et seq.). The story of the oil is found in the Talmud (*c.* fourth century C.E.).

Location

Originally Jerusalem and the Temple. Now principally in the home.

Ritual

The principal ritual of the festival is the lighting of the chanukiyah. This is ideally outside, but it is usually placed in a window. Soon after sunset the shamash (servant light) is lit with a match. Then it is used to light the other candles (or oil lights). One extra candle is lit each night. On the first night the candle on the far right is lit. On the second night the second from the right is lit first, followed by the first candle from the right. This continues for eight nights until the whole chanukiyah is lit up. After this the following prayer is said:

... these lights are sacred, neither is it permitted us to make any profane use of them; but we are only to look at them, in order that we may give thanks unto thy name for thy miracles, thy deliverance and they wonders.

Siddur

Chanukah songs such as *Hanerot Halalu* and *Ma'oz Tzur* are sung. (*Living Festivals – Chanukah*, p. 9.) The

Hallel prayer is recited during the festival and the *Al Hanissim* prayer is inserted into the Grace.

Often children are given coins as presents. These are known as *Chanukah Gelt* and represent the first coins struck by the Maccabees when they repossessed the city. Children play with dreidels.

Artefacts

The nine-branched candelabrum, the *Chanukah menorah* or *chanukiyah*. It has eight lights plus one called the *shamash* – the slave. The Chanukah lights must not be used for any purpose other than to publicize the festival so therefore one cannot be used to light another. The shamash is used to light the actual Chanukah candles.

Dreidel (in Hebrew *svivon*) – this is a four-sided top. (*Living Festivals – Chanukah*, p. 10.)

On each face is a Hebrew character:

נ   nun

ג   gimmel

ה   heh

ש   shin

They stand for the phrase *Nes gadol haya sham* – a great miracle happened there.

They also represent the Yiddish words

nichts	(take) nothing
ganz	(take) all
halb	(take) half
shtell ein	put one in

A game can be played with the dreidel. In this game, counters are put into or removed from a central pool according to the face on which the dreidel falls. Tradition says that the game was played by Jewish children when they were studying Torah and were discovered by Greeks.

Food

Traditional food is that which is fried in oil. It reminds Jews of the miracle in the Temple. This is represented by potato cakes – latkes (Hebrew – levivot) – for Ashkenazim, and for Sefardim, especially in Israel, doughnuts.

Significant Persons

Mattathias, Judah the Maccabee, Antiochus IV.

THEMES FOR THE CLASSROOM

1 Perhaps the most obvious theme to be drawn from this festival is that of light. Chanukah is sometimes called the *Festival of Lights* because of the significance of the lighting of the chanukiyah.

2 It would then be worthwhile looking at the importance of the symbol of light and seeing how various religions attach importance to light. There was no suggestion that Chanukah was connected with a winter festival of light looking forward to the longer days of Spring until the sixteenth century and the work of Rabbi Judah Loeb.

However, festivals of light do tend to be celebrated in the winter and teachers might wish to look at Divali and Christmas in this context.

3 The triumph of good over evil is represented here but, perhaps more important, the way in which a small group of people on the side of what is right can successfully challenge a larger and stronger body who are in the wrong; the ideas of faith and determination.

4 Jews are not permitted to work by the lights of the chanukiyah as its importance is to advertise the great event in the Temple. Christianity has long displayed itself in public and, perhaps regrettably, has been adopted in a very commercial way at Christmas and Easter. The point to be made is how should people make a public display of their faith and why intolerance and prejudice acts against religions, bearing in mind that in the past many Jews were forced to hide their chanukiyah rather than have it on public display. What stance should religious people take over these issues?

4 With older pupils a study of Chanukah affords an opportunity to look beyond the traditional canon of the Bible and consider the Apochryphal works such as the Book of Maccabees.

THE WORKSHEETS

The first worksheet is designed to produce the story of Chanukah retold in cartoon form.

The next worksheet contains instructions for making a chanukiyah.

There is a Wordsquare and Wordsearch on the subject of Chanukah and finally a test and full assessment.

CHANUKAH CARTOON

Plan out a one-page cartoon strip version of the story of Chanukah to fit in the boxes below. Draw brightly coloured pictures in the large boxes. Use the small boxes for the story-line or dialogue. You can also use speech bubbles for what people say and sound effects like ZAP! or POW!

THE STORY OF CHANUKAH

MAKING A CHANUKIYAH

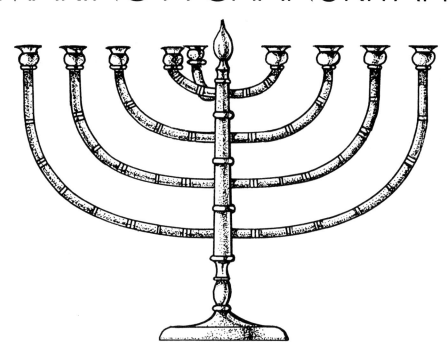

Many chanukiyot are very beautiful and families treasure them as they are passed down from generation to generation.

These instructions are for making a very simple chanukiyah but you may be able to think of another way of making and decorating this nine-branched candlestick.

MATERIALS

piece of wood approx. 25 cm × 30 mm × 30 mm
9 small foil cake cases
9 drawing-pins
9 candles
acrylic paints or felt-tip pens

1 Divide the length of the wood into eight sections approx. 3 cm long. One of the end sections should be a little longer than the others, approx. 4 cm.

2 Pin one foil case at each point marked along the wood and one at each end.

3 Shape the cases to hold the candles (the servant candle stands at one end a little way from the others).

4 Decorate the wood with paints or felt-tip pens. You can use patterns or Jewish symbols in your decoration.

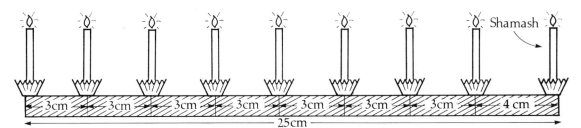

CHANUKAH WORDSQUARE

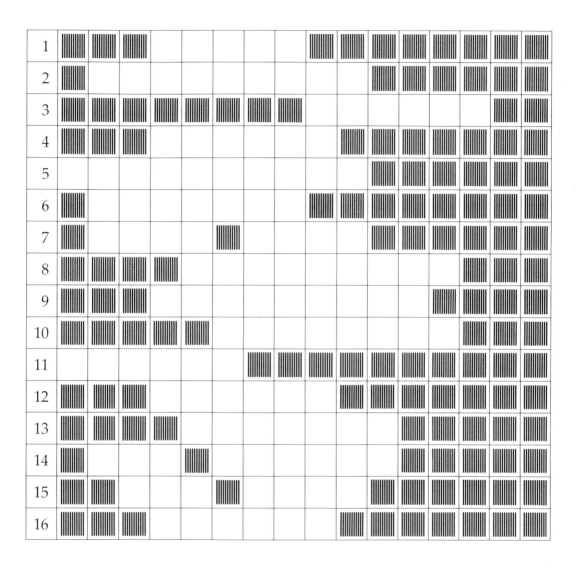

1 He was a leader of the Jewish people at this time

2 The group of men were called the M_____

3 They wanted to recapture the T_____

4 ... which had been taken by the G_____

5 At this time people light a C_____

6 The eight candles are lit by the S_____

7 One of the Chanukah songs is M_____ T_____

8 The story of this struggle is in the book of the M_____

9 The Jews were fighting the men led by A_____

10 Children play a game with D_____ at this time

11 ... and people eat L_____

12 It is in the month of K_____

13 Number 5 has 9 branches, a M_____ has seven

14 In Hebrew: a great miracle N_____ G_____

15 ... happened here H_____ S_____

16 This is sometimes called a festival of L_____

CHANUKAH WORDSEARCH

Z	T	H	C	I	N	O	J	A	R	U	D	D	I	S	D	E
A	R	P	C	H	A	N	U	K	A	H	O	H	N	U	N	L
P	O	Z	N	A	G	G	D	E	S	T	E	O	M	A	B	E
U	S	N	A	S	I	U	A	B	V	H	A	L	B	R	E	M
L	A	I	N	M	S	H	H	O	U	N	A	B	R	O	K	M
A	I	D	T	O	E	L	P	M	E	T	D	M	A	S	H	I
L	H	O	I	N	A	N	P	O	A	S	E	R	A	D	F	G
A	T	M	O	E	D	F	O	G	A	C	R	T	Y	S	E	S
H	A	E	C	A	S	I	V	R	U	R	C	T	C	A	H	E
T	T	L	H	N	L	S	E	E	A	B	A	A	S	D	A	K
O	T	D	U	S	E	L	L	E	T	H	S	W	B	O	L	T
R	A	N	S	Y	N	E	S	K	A	T	H	G	I	E	L	A
E	M	A	S	I	J	K	I	S	E	D	R	E	I	D	E	L
N	O	C	H	A	N	U	K	I	Y	A	H	E	E	R	L	O
A	S	S	U	T	M	A	O	Z	T	Z	U	R	D	F	V	Y
H	A	P	O	C	R	Y	P	H	A	S	S	T	H	G	I	L

CHANUKAH	DREIDEL	HEH
TALMUD	MA'OZ TZUR	HALB
CHANUKIYAH	LATKES	SACRED
SHAMASH	GIMMEL	TEMPLE
CANDLE	GANZ	OIL
APOCRYPHA	GREEKS	MACCABEE
NUN	MENORAH	EIGHT
NICHTZ	MATTATHIAS	SIDDUR
KORBAN	KISLEV	MODIN
HASMONEANS	ANTIOCHUS	SHIN
HALLEL	HANEROT HALALU	SHTELL
JUDAH	LIGHTS	

CHANUKAH TEST

1 Why is this festival sometimes called a **Festival of Light**?

2 Describe the **lighting** of the chanukiyah.

3 Why does a Chanukah menorah have nine branches instead of the usual seven?

4 Why did the Jews have to clean and rededicate the **Temple**?

5 Who was the **Jewish leader** at this time?

6 The **story** of Chanukah is not found in the Bible. Where is it?

7 What is **Chanukah Gelt**?

8 What is a **dreidel** and how is it used?

9 Why are **latkes** and **doughnuts** traditional foods for this festival?

10 Why do you think the Chanukah menorah has to be **outside** or in a window?

CHANUKAH ASSESSMENT

1 What does **Chanukah** celebrate?

2 When does it take place?

3 Give **TWO** reasons for the festival lasting **eight days**?

4 What is the significance of the **chanukiyah** and of **latkes** and **doughnuts** at Chanukah?

5 Why do you think Chanukah is sometimes called the **'Jewish Christmas'**? Why should it **never** be referred to in this way?

6 Why must the light of the candles **not be used to work by**?

7 Why do many Jews feel that they **cannot** obey the instruction to display their chanukiyah in a window during the festival?

8 Describe the **struggle of the Maccabees**?

9 What reason is sometimes given for the development of the **dreidel**?

10 What do the **letters** on a dreidel stand for?

11 What is **Chanukah Gelt** and what does it represent?

12 What is the **importance of the phrase**, 'Not by might, nor by power, but by My Spirit, saith the Lord of hosts'?

13 Although the story of the rededication of the Temple is found in the Book of Maccabees, where would you find the story of the **miracle of the oil**?

Tu B'Shevat

INTRODUCTION

Jews of the Diaspora have celebrated *Tu B'Shevat* – New Year for Trees – for 2000 years.

Stories and Legends

It is a Rabbinic festival mentioned in the Talmud and celebrated on 15 Shevat.

The day marks the time when the sap begins to rise in fruit trees in Israel and was a day for tithing fruit. Any fruit which blossoms after this day belongs to the next year for tithing. It was also the time for deciding the laws for the Sabbatical Year. This institution, ordered by Leviticus 25, required that for one year in every seven, the land should be left to lie fallow and all debtors and Jewish slaves were to be freed.

Sources

Talmud.

Location

Israel and the Diaspora.

Ritual

People also send money to the Jewish National Fund to buy a tree which will be planted in Israel. Penitential prayers are omitted from the liturgy for the day and fasting is forbidden.

Artefacts

Trees (saplings) and fruit.

Food

Jews in the Diaspora celebrate this by eating fruits from Israel such as bokser, carob fruit, almonds (15 kinds if possible as this is the fifteenth day of the month).

Significant Persons

Everyone.

THEMES FOR THE CLASSROOM

There is little obvious work that can be built up around this festival but it does present an opportunity to study the Sabbatical Year and also the importance of trees in the Torah. In the Psalms there are occasions where a fruit-laden tree is compared to a person who does good deeds.

However, there is an opportunity here to set up cross-curricular work with History and Geography on the State of Israel past and present and modern methods of farming and reclaiming the land. The money sent to plant new trees every year plays an important part in this.

Perhaps the moral/ecological idea of *not* plundering the land could also be developed with pupils.

THE WORKSHEETS

As there is no *Living Festivals* pupils' book to cover this festival there is simply a full assessment on the importance of Tu B'Shevat.

TU B'SHEVAT ASSESSMENT

1 Describe fully what this festival **celebrates**?

2 When does it **take place**?

3 How is **Tu B'Shevat celebrated today**?

4 What was the importance of the **Sabbatical Year**?

5 What is **forbidden** on this day?

6 What do people in the Diaspora traditionally **eat** on this day?

7 What **special significance** does the celebration of this festival have for the State of Israel today?

8 What **lessons** could people in the rest of the world learn from this celebration?

Purim

INTRODUCTION

Purim, the Feast of Lots, is celebrated on 14 Adar. The day before is *Ta'anit Esther*, the Fast of Esther.

Purim is the happiest holiday of the Jewish calendar but an old saying is

a headache is not an illness and Purim is not a Yom Tov.

However, this does not prevent the day being celebrated with great enthusiasm.

Stories and Legends

The retelling of the story of Esther is the main event of the day.

In the fifth century B.C.E. the Jews of Persia were ruled by King Ahasuerus. Haman, his prime minister, was an anti-Semite who was angered by Mordecai, a Jew who refused to bow down to him. Mordecai's niece, Esther, was Ahasuerus' wife although no one apart from Mordecai knew that she was a Jewess.

Haman ordered the destruction of the Jews in Persia. Mordecai asked Esther for help. She arranged a party for Haman and the king but lost her nerve. She also said that she and all other Jews should fast for three days. The next day she arranged another party and told the king everything about herself and about Haman. Ahasuerus was angry at Haman's plans. He rewarded Mordecai and ordered the execution of Haman and his ten sons on the gallows that were being built for Mordecai.

Mordecai wrote to other Jewish communities telling them to celebrate on 14 Adar. He told them to send gifts to each other and to the poor. The name *Purim* means 'lottery' because Haman drew number 14 – the day he was to be killed.

Sources

Book of Esther, written about 460 B.C.E.

Location

The story of Esther takes place in the city of Shushan in Persia.

The modern celebration takes place primarily in the synagogue but often festivities and celebrations move out into the streets.

However, like other Jewish festivals, much of the preparation is in the home.

Ritual

There are several rituals associated with the festival.

The Fast of Esther is a minor fast to remember that made by Esther herself. It lasts only from dawn to dusk on the day preceding Purim.

Four rituals are mitzvot:

1 *Shalach manot* or *Mishloach manot* – this is the obligation imposed by Mordecai to:

make the fourteenth day of the month of Adar a day of gladness and feasting, and a good day, and of sending portions one to another.

Esther 9:19

This has been interpreted as meaning that everyone must send at least *two* gifts of food or drink to at least one person.

2 *Matanot La'evyonim* – again this is a requirement of Mordecai:

and gifts to the poor.

Esther 9:22

Therefore Jews send gifts, usually of money, to the poor for Purim.

3 The third mitzvah is to hear the *Megillah* – the scroll of Esther – being read. When the *Maariv* prayer is sung after dusk it is done as a parody using melodies belonging to other festivals. This is followed by the reading of the Megillah. This scroll is on only one wooden roller and is opened out then folded like Mordecai's letters ordering all other Jews to celebrate the festival.

The reading is a humorous event. Often the reader will change voices for the characters or dress up to play the parts. Every time that the name of Haman is mentioned there is booing, the rattling of greggers (football rattles), and the stamping of shoes, on the soles of which are written Haman's name. The atmosphere is a carnival one and afterwards there are often carnival parties and dances.

The mitzvah is to hear the Megillah twice and people return to the synagogue in the morning.

4 The fourth mitzvah is the *seudah*, the Purim feast which ends the day. There is no ritual attached to this; it is a good meal with plenty to drink. People sing traditional songs such as *Shoshannat Yaakov*.

Some Jews serve dishes of vegetables at this meal to remind themselves that Esther avoided eating non-kosher meat in the palace.

Parties are a vital part of the celebrations because the word *mishteh*, a feast, occurs twenty times in the Book of Esther. People are encouraged, on this one occasion of the year, to drink sufficient that they do not know the difference between 'Blessed be Mordecai' and 'Cursed be Haman'.

A final feature of the day in some communities is the *shpeel* or Purim play. This is a satirical event when pupils make fun of their teachers and elect a Purim Rabbi.

Artefacts
Megillah – scroll of Esther.
Greggers, whistles, etc.

Food
Food and drink are an important ingredient of the day especially for the seudah. The traditional Purim food is Hamantaschen – three-cornered pastries filled with poppy seeds. The word means 'Haman's pockets' but they are sometimes said to represent his three-cornered hat.

In some Arab communities where they received presents from Jewish neighbours, the festival was known as Eid al-Sukar – 'the festival of sugar' – because of these sweet foods which were eaten.

Significant Persons
Mordecai, Esther, Haman, Ahasuerus.

THEMES FOR THE CLASSROOM

There are four major themes which the story of Purim suggests for the classroom:

1 The need to be faithful and true to what you believe, and to have courage and trust that if you are honest and stand up for what is right you will ultimately triumph. There are several points which can be made on this in the discussion of Purim:
   (a) Mordecai refuses to bow down to the evil Haman because of his religious beliefs and therefore risks his life, but eventually he is vindicated.
   (b) Esther initially has hidden the fact that she is Jewish from everyone including her husband, but when it appears that her uncle and many other people will die unless she speaks up she risks the consequences and again is vindicated by her husband's actions.
   (c) Haman appears to be almost totally wicked and so receives his just punishment for his in-human intentions.

2 The idea that it is right to be happy and celebrate religious events like this. It makes the point that despite all the sufferings of the Jews they are able to celebrate Purim every year in a carnival atmosphere and without solemnity. They do this in order to fulfill the mitzvah, and also simply to have a good time with their families, friends and neighbours. A possible disaster is turned into an occasion for celebrating the triumph of good over evil.

3 The age-old idea of the triumph of good over evil is very clearly presented there.

4 The idea contained in the mitzvah of Mordecai's letter that provision should be made for the less fortunate to celebrate the festivities as well.

Finally, the idea of the carnival atmosphere and the shpeel might suggest some cross-religious work on the concept of Carnival and Misrule.

THE WORKSHEETS

The first worksheet is a piece of cloze work on the story of Purim. The second is to prepare pupils for writing a shpeel or Purim play. There are instructions for making a gregger and then a game based on the festival story.

There is a Wordsquare and Wordsearch on the festival and finally a test and full assessment.

THE STORY OF PURIM

Fill in the gaps in this passage using the words at the bottom of the page.

In the fifth century B.C.E. the Jews of Persia were ruled by King＿＿＿＿＿＿ . Haman, his prime minster, hated the Jews and was angered by＿＿＿＿＿＿, a Jew who refused to bow down to him. Mordecai's niece,＿＿＿＿＿＿, was Ahasuerus' wife although no one except Mordecai knew that she was a ＿＿＿＿＿.

Haman ordered the death of the Jews in ＿＿＿＿＿. Mordecai asked Esther for help. She arranged a ＿＿＿＿＿ for Haman and the king but lost her nerve. She also said that she and all other Jews should ＿＿＿＿ for ＿＿＿＿days. The next day she arranged another party and told the king everything about herself and about Haman. Ahasuerus was ＿＿＿＿＿ at Haman's plans. He rewarded Mordecai and ordered the＿＿＿＿＿of Haman and his ten ＿＿＿＿ on the ＿＿＿＿＿ that were being built for Mordecai.

Mordecai wrote to other ＿＿＿＿＿ communities telling them to celebrate on ＿＿＿＿＿. He told them to send ＿＿＿＿ to each other and to the poor. The name *Purim* means ＿＿＿＿＿ because Haman drew number 14 – the day he was to be killed.

Esther	**Jewish**	**Persia**	**Jewess**
execution	Ahasuerus	Mordecai	gallows
sons	party	angry	gifts
three	lottery	fast	14 Adar

THE SHPEEL

The **shpeel** or **Purim play** is a very popular part of celebrations for the festival.

You will find the story of Purim in the Bible in the **Book of Esther**.

You are going to **write** and **perform** a **Purim play**.

Remember that although the threat to the Jews of this time was very serious, the important thing about the festival is that it is **fun**.

The main characters will be **Esther**, **Haman**, **Mordecai** and **Ahaseurus**.

Make sure that your audience have **whistles** and **greggers** and know that they have to cheer and shout **'Blessed be Mordecai'** and **'Cursed be Haman'**.

Your costumes and make-up should be as **funny as possible**. Do not try to use Biblical language for the characters. Instead use modern everyday English.

You do not need to write down the words. If everyone knows the story well you can improvise it or else the characters can mime to a reading.

A GREGGER

MATERIALS

two large foil pie or cake cases (approx. 10 cm in diameter)
handful of dried peas
piece of thin dowel approx. 20 cm long
stapler
acrylic paint

1 Place the peas in one of the cases.
2 Place the second case over the first.
3 Staple the edges of the cases together leaving a small gap on either side.
4 Insert the dowel through the holes and secure it with staples to form a handle.
5 Paint the case with a picture of Haman or write 'Cursed be Haman' on it.

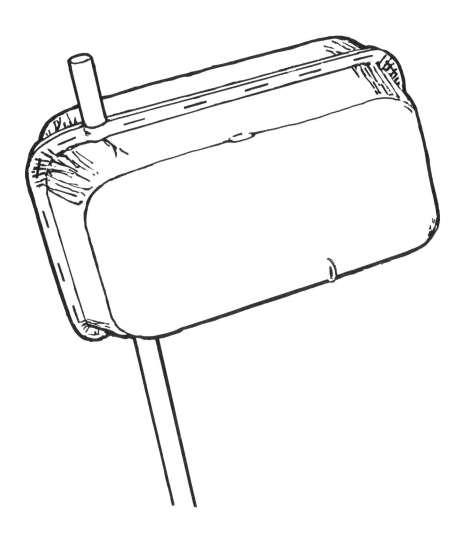

PURIM GAME

The aim of the game is to be the first person to reach 14 Adar. Throw a **three** to be the first to start. You must throw exactly the right number to land on 54. There are seven squares with the names of objects on them and you gain 5 points for each one you land on. You get 50 points for finishing so the winner is the person to finish with most points.

1 Start	2	3 Eat sweets **Back 2**	4	5 GREGGER	6 Talk with Mordecai **Miss a turn**
26 Whistle **On 2**	27	28	29 Mordecai writes a letter **Miss a turn**	30 MEGILLAH	7
25 HATS	44	45	46 Ahaseurus listens **Miss a turn**	31	8
24	43 Build gallows **Back 20**	54 **14 Adar**	47	32 Eat with Haman **Back 5**	9 Give to the poor **On 5**
23 Listen to Megillah **On 4**	42	53 Haman interferes **Back 4**	48 Break gregger **Miss a turn**	33	10 WHISTLE
22 Make gregger **On 3**	41	52	49 Eat Seudah (a mitzvah) **On 2**	34 Make Haman- taschen **Miss a turn**	11
21	40 Mordecai writes a letter **Miss a turn**	51 Esther fasts **On 1**	50	35 HAMAN- TASCHEN	12 Drink **Miss 2 turns**
20 FOOD	39	38 Fold Megillah **On 3**	37	36 Stamp shoes **On 3**	13
19 Mordecai writes a letter **Miss a turn**	18	17	16 Give food **On 4**	15 SHOES	14 Prepare Seudah **Miss a turn**

PURIM WORDSQUARE

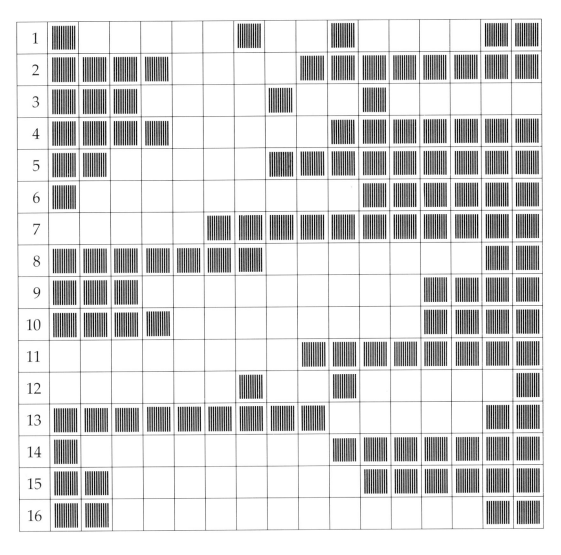

1 Purim is also called the F_____ of L_____

2 It takes place during the month of A_____

3 The story is found in the B_____ of E_____

4 It tells how the wicked H _____ tried to have all the Jews in Persia killed

5 Mordecai's niece E_____ was married

6 to King A_____

7 For T_____ days she fasted

8 and persuaded her husband to send Haman to the G_____ instead of Mordecai

9 The story is read in the S_____

10 from a special scroll called a M _____

11 While it is being read, people shout 'Blessed be M_____

12 and 'C_____ be H _____'

13 They S_____ their feet

14 blow W_____

15 and rattle G _____

16 Special cakes called H _____ are eaten

91

PURIM WORDSEARCH

V	C	S	K	N	I	R	D	M	I	S	H	T	E	H	R	A
O	U	T	A	B	G	P	U	R	I	M	M	I	S	H	E	S
K	R	A	B	C	E	O	N	S	T	O	L	N	A	A	G	H
A	S	M	N	R	E	P	A	G	U	R	T	A	B	D	G	A
Y	E	P	S	A	A	P	M	R	E	D	S	A	S	U	E	L
Y	D	I	C	W	H	Y	A	T	E	E	S	T	H	E	R	A
T	A	N	U	E	W	S	H	A	H	C	V	P	P	S	G	C
A	E	G	A	R	A	K	U	S	L	A	D	I	E	D	A	H
N	H	S	S	W	E	E	T	H	T	I	M	Y	E	E	S	M
N	A	W	I	S	U	R	E	U	S	A	H	A	L	S	S	A
A	L	O	T	T	E	R	Y	B	A	S	D	V	N	S	E	N
H	L	L	S	T	A	M	P	P	F	A	E	V	E	E	L	O
S	I	L	T	E	K	C	O	P	R	A	Q	W	O	L	T	T
O	G	A	N	T	I	S	E	M	I	T	E	P	I	B	T	V
H	E	G	E	L	T	S	I	H	W	J	S	E	C	N	A	D
S	M	A	H	A	M	A	N	T	A	S	C	H	E	N	R	A

SWEET
ESTHER
SHPEEL
AHASUERUS
YAKOV
ADAR
JEWESS
MANOT
HAMANTASCHEN
EID AL SUKAR
STAMP
HAMAN
DRINK

ANTI-SEMITE
POPPY
TAANIT
MISHTEH
BLESSED
RATTLES
CURSED
PURIM
LOTS
WHISTLE
FAST
SHALACH
LOTTERY

HAT
GREGGER
SEUDAH
MORDECAI
SHOSHANNAT
PERSIA
GALLOWS
DANCES
SHUSHAN
POCKET
MEGILLAH
STAMPING

PURIM TEST

1 What **other names** does Purim have?

2 What is the **day before** Purim called?

3 In your own words tell the **story** of Purim.

4 What is the **main event** of the day's celebrations called?

5 What is a **Megillah**?

6 What **gifts** have to be given at Purim?

7 Imagine that you have been to a **reading in a synagogue** at Purim. Try to describe the experience in writing.

8 Draw a **picture** or design a **poster** for Purim.

9 What are **Hamantaschen** and why are they called by this name?

10 What is a **shpeel**?

11 What are the main points of the character of **Esther**. Is she a good example for us all? Why?/Why not?

PURIM ASSESSMENT

1 When does Purim **take place**?

2 Why is the day before Purim a **day of fasting**?

3 Try to explain the saying *'A headache is not an illness and Purim is not a Yom Tov'*.

4 Name **THREE** of the four **mitzvot** or commandments associated with Purim.

5 In what ways is the reading of the **Megillah** different from usual synagogue services?

6 How is the way the Megillah is treated and handled very different from the treatment of the **Torah scrolls**?

7 What does the word **Purim** mean?

8 What **TWO** phrases are **shouted** during the Megillah reading?

9 Why have some Muslims described Purim as **Eid al-Sukar**?

10 What are the main points of the **story of Esther**?

11 What are the main teachings about **right and wrong** in this story?

12 Why might it be though **odd** that the Jews, of all religious groups, should celebrate a festival in this way? Give reasons for your answer.

Resources

Books for pupils
LIVING FESTIVALS SERIES
Chanukah, L. Scholefield. R.M.E.P., 1983.
Passover, L. Scholefield. R.M.E.P., 1982.
Rosh Hashanah and Yom Kippur. F. Gent. R.M.E.P., 1988.
Shabbat, C. Bryan and V. Whitburn. R.M.E.P., 1985.
Succot and Simchat Torah, L. Scholefield. R.M.E.P., 1987.

Exploring the Bible, Book 1, Founders to Judges, A. Goldstein. R.M.E.P., 1987.
Exploring the Bible, Book 2, The Monarchy to the Exile, A. Goldstein. R.M.E.P., 1988.
Feasting and Fasting, John Mayled. Wayland, 1986.
Festive Occasions, J. Ridgeway. OUP, 1986.
A Jewish Family in Britain, V. Barnett. R.M.E.P., 1983.
Judaism in Words and Pictures, S. Thorley. R.M.E.P., 1986.
Religious Festivals, Jon Mayled. Wayland, 1987.
Soul Cakes and Shish Kebabs. A Multifaith Cookery Book, Aviva Paraïso and Jon Mayled. R.M.E.P., 1988.

Books for teachers
Festivals in World Religions, SHAP. Longman, 1986.
How to Run a Traditional Jewish Household, B. Greenberg. Simon & Schuster Inc., 1983.

The Jewish Catalog, Jewish Publication Society of America, Philadelphia, 1973.
Jews: Their Religious Beliefs and Practices, A. Unterman. Routledge & Kegan Paul, 1981.

Videos
All the following are available from Pergamon Educational Productions (PEP), Hennock Road, Exeter EX2 8RP.

LIVING FESTIVALS SERIES
Living Festivals Video 1. PEP, 1987.
Living Festivals Video 2. PEP, 1987.

Aspects of Judaism. Videotext, Exmouth, 1983.
Judaism through the eyes of Jewish Children. PEP, 1985.
Looking at Faith Programme 1. PEP, 1986.

Posters
Pictorial Charts Educational Trust.

Computer programs
A computer program is available for the IBM PC[TM] and compatibles to convert between the Jewish and Gregorian calendars. Further details can be obtained from the publisher.

Index of Worksheets